THE MEDALLION

A NOVEL

Patrick Olesko

PAGE PUBLISHING
Conneaut Lake, PA

First originally published by Page Publishing 2023

ISBN 979-8-88793-367-2 (pbk)
ISBN 979-8-88793-377-1 (digital)

Printed in the United States of America

CHAPTER 1

Jessie parked her car behind her husband's matching silver BMW. She sat for a moment staring at the portico of their home. Purchased only four months earlier, it had taken on a sinister air, and now sitting inside the car, staring up at the grand facade, the hair on her arms began to rise, and she felt an eerie and familiar chill come over her.

Located in the center of the circular drive, the bubbling of the three-tiered fountain capped off with a cement pineapple once soothed her after a hectic day. Pineapples were considered age-old symbols of welcome and hospitality dating as far back as the sixteenth century. But this one, dribbling rivulets of water to the tiers below, gave her no sense of welcome, let alone hospitality. Now its splattering had become nothing more than a disturbing din.

Her mind returned to her husband's vehicle. *There was an attached three-car garage, why did he choose to park it right out in front?* she wondered. Maybe he had forgotten something, returned home, and quickly ran in to retrieve whatever it was. But her senses told her differently. It's the middle of the afternoon. He never gets home until late. And he is a highly organized person. He would and has never left the house forgetting anything.

She climbed out of her car, closed the door quietly, so as not to alert anyone that she had arrived. She found the door key in her Coach handbag and wondered why she was being so suspicious. Negative thoughts had become a daily occurrence since their move in. The hairs on her arms, and now, those on the back of her neck were at full alert. In fact, she made a habit of shopping or lunching with friends more often so she could avoid being in the house.

Ascending the two steps onto the portico, she ignored the stately columns carved in the Doric style similar to those of the Greek Parthenon. The house, erected only ten years earlier, evoked both modern affluence with a pinch of old southern charm. Trepidation continued to fill her. Nothing was the same after their first couple of days. In fact, after a few weeks, she referred to it as "a house," never "a home."

In those first days, she would sometimes linger before going inside, often affectionately caressing the surface of a column, as though it were a beloved member of the family. And when she approached the grand French doors, ten feet in height, she did so with an exhilaration of a queen entering her palace. She realized it was all silliness, that they were just the entry to their new home. But no matter how *Gone with the Wind* Tara it appeared on the outside, inside it was their mini mansion offering every amenity anyone could ever want. Ultra-modern kitchen, granite counters, a Viking range, a walk-in wine closet with racks for hundreds of bottles, a formal dining room that could host at least twenty, an office, a huge laundry room, and outside, a swimming pool, a patio barbeque, showers, and toilets. Upstairs, four enormous bedrooms, each with a private bathroom, and a master bedroom with matching his-and-her bathrooms and more closet space than they could ever use. And so much land! They were virtually isolated from any other homes that might be in the area. In fact, no other buildings existed on Hawk's Bend. This was the only one. Secluded and private. And when they heard the asking price, they were astounded. So little for so much! Their real estate agent, Loretta, had said something about the sellers, a family of five, needing to leave quickly and just to get the house sold as soon as possible. Even her husband, who haggled about anything bearing a dollar sign couldn't believe their luck.

Now her fingers trembled as she inserted the key into the lock, pushed open the door, and stepped into the foyer. Once she had been seized by the exquisite gleaming beauty of the Italian marble beneath her feet, the gilded-framed mirrors aligning the walls, the windows the height of two floors that should be filtering in the natural sunlight. Even the hundreds of crystals dangling from the chandelier above could not evict the interior drear. No matter how bright and sunlit it might be outdoors, inside it was always gloomy. The house had lost its welcome. It was becoming a dark and oppressive prison.

She set her handbag on the foyer table, remembering to remove her cell phone, slipping it into the pocket of her designer jeans.

"Peter?" she called out, her thoughts returning to the unknown whereabouts of her husband. Her voice echoed off the hard surfaces of stone and wood. The only other sound was the clicking of her Manolo heels against the marble tiles. No answer. *That's odd*, she thought.

She peeked into the room just to the left, Peter's private office. No one. The desk light was out, the computer screen dark. She then proceeded into the cavernous kitchen. The silence seemed to intensify around her. There was not a sound except for the hum of the refrigerator and the clicks of her heels. Everything was neat and orderly just as it had been before she left for a day of shopping. That ruled out Peter having an afternoon snack. If he had, dirty dishes and utensils would be in the sink or just left on the table for her to clean up. As organized as he was, he was useless at kitchen chores. The silence continued to grow, as if it were attempting to consume her.

Finding her way to the back of the house, she entered the family room, or "rec" room, as Peter referred to it. The sofa was empty, the wide screen television affixed to the wall was off. There was no one. She turned to peer out the floor to ceiling windows. Scanning the patio, past the pool, down the lawn that went on seemingly forever, to the clump of wild thickets beyond, a wall of assorted palms and bramble that encircled the huge yard, a barrier to the swamp behind. Although she had never had the courage to venture that far to even see it—it seemed wild and dangerous.

The sky was cloudless, the afternoon sun bright, the outside air crystal clear, quite unlike the suffocating gloom of the indoor atmosphere. Nevertheless, it was an unusually perfect Florida winter day, an enticement to steal a nap. But no one idled poolside. Besides, Peter was not one to laze around when he could be at his home office or the downtown office, overseeing his four employees, all peddling insurance of every kind, making money. Something he not only enjoyed but also was talented at doing. The mystery of his whereabouts only deepened as did her concerns.

Returning to the foyer, her apprehension grew as she stepped upon the bottom tread of the grand staircase, hesitating to call out his name again. Still nothing. Something wasn't right, she could sense it. Her gut told her, the hair on her neck told her. An unusual energy in the house concurred.

Slowly, she began the climb, pausing every two steps, calling out, waiting—hoping—for a response. None came. No sound of the television, nor the shower running nor the toilet flushing. Nothing. A sensation of dread fell over her. She crept along the hall, freezing in mid-step. All the family photos—happy photos of their European travels, wild elephants from the safari they had taken not long ago, and photos taken of the Asian jungles from the deck of their river-boat voyage—all were now hanging upside down. Odd and frightening events such as this had been occurring more frequently. First, it was just little things: the tapping; the scratching; objects moving or disappearing completely; the unexplained humanlike shadows looming darkly against the walls. In the last couple of days, she had felt a shift. An intensification of energy. The house was coming alive. She had experienced fear before, but not like this: blood-chilling. Her breath quickened, she moved faster to the master bedroom.

"Peter?" she called out.

She heard gasping, as if someone were being strangled. She quickened her pace.

She pushed open the door and froze.

Peter, in bed, naked except for the socks on his feet, struggling against the fingers gripping his throat.

Above him, Jessie made out a black amorphous form, a dark mist, hovering above her husband. What appeared to be hands reached out to grip his neck. She could see it was trying to strangle him. Little gurgles came from his constricted throat. A cold terror, the likes of which she had never felt before, ripped through her body. Her heart pounded. A shriek exploded from her throat.

The creature turned its head in her direction. It slowly lifted from Peter's paralyzed body and stood, facing Jesse. Now its features slowly became more solid, more identifiable.

Jesse saw it was female. A long tangle of matted black hair reached to her shoulders, skin, the color of mahogany, mutilated by pock marks, glared at her. Its eyes glowed with such hate and anger Jessie had never before felt from anyone. Covering her breast hung a plate made of assorted shells. She could make out nothing below the waist, no hips, legs, or feet. The creature just floated free of any earthly restraints, hovering, directing all its evil intent toward Jessie.

It moved closer. Jessie stood, frozen with fear. Yet she managed to take a step back, pressing her back against the door jamb, creating more space between her and that thing. It approached, closer and closer, so close that Jessie could now feel its cold fetid breath on her cheeks. Jessie thought she would vomit both from the foul odor and from her own terror.

With a heart pounding so hard, so hard that it might fly from her chest, she closed her eyes so as not to see what it would do to her. She would have to let fate takes its course. Helpless, all she could do was to release another blood curdling shriek.

The air in the room suddenly changed. It became lighter, warmer. She opened her eyes. The thing had disappeared.

Peter leapt from the bed, found his bathrobe, and ran to his wife.

"My God!" was all he could find to say. He massaged his throat where stinging red handprints had appeared.

Still trembling, her pulse still pounding, she managed to retrieve the cell phone from her pocket.

"Who are you calling?" Peter asked, disbelieving that she would think to call anyone at this moment.

He moved toward her, but Jessie placed the palm of her hand against his chest and gently pushed him back. She felt her fear slowly evolving into anger.

After three rings, Loretta picked up.

"This is Jessie Magrew. You know, we bought the place on Hawk's Bend about four months go?" Her hand shook, her voice trembled, and she had difficulty holding onto the phone. "Could you please put the house up for sale? Peter and I have decided to move out. We're leaving this afternoon. Take whatever you can get for it. At a loss if need be. I'll have our lawyer handle everything. He'll call you very soon."

Jessie paused as Loretta spoke.

"The reasons don't matter. Just sell it as soon as possible."

She terminated the call and replaced the phone into her pocket. Then looking at Peter, she said, "We can't go on like this."

Her husband saw how ashen her complexion had become. Her hands still shook. In the four months living in the house, this had been the worst experience. They stood quietly embracing each other, as if their lives depended upon it. They were not safe at night nor, after this experience, by day.

"I just can't take it anymore," she said. "I don't care if we move into a shed with an outhouse!"

"I know," he said, surprised that his class-conscious wife would even suggest such a thing. "Why didn't you just tell Loretta the reason?"

Jessie looked at him incredulously. "You think she'd believe everything that's been going on in here? The footsteps, the shadow people, the whispering in the middle of the night? What just happened to you!? And your headaches! Those began as soon as we moved in here."

Peter had to agree. "That's why I came home so early. I thought I'd feel better if I took a nap."

"And what about us?" She continued. "We have never had a serious argument in our twenty years of marriage. The dream couple, everyone called us. Now we're at it like cats and dogs!" She glanced around the room. "This was to be our dream home. But it's turned into a nightmare. A goddam nightmare!" Tears began to stream from her eyes.

"Loretta would think we were nuts if I told her everything that's been going on in here." Jessie added: "Anyone would. Who knows? Maybe we are."

"We're not nuts," Peter assured her, placing one of his hands on her left shoulder while the other wiped the moisture accumulating upon her cheeks. "Come on, let's pull it together and pack up some suitcases. We'll get a hotel room, and tomorrow we'll start looking for another place, maybe just a rental for now. On the north side of town. Away from here."

She managed a smile. "Thanks," she said as she leaned in and kissed him.

CHAPTER 2

Loretta slowly drove her blue Honda along Hawk's Bend Road as her client, Christine Minter, admired the passing Florida landscape.

She really had no desire to show this property to anyone in the three months since the Magrews abandoned it, and she was surprised that some other agent had not already sold it. But here it was—still on the market.

Besides, there was just something about the place she did not like and with the mysterious departure of now three owners, she'd rather let the place rot. But the Magrews' lawyer had been after her to unload it so everyone could "move on," as he put it. Nevertheless, when Christine called and told Loretta that she, her husband Stan, and their two children were moving down from upstate New York to relocate to this part of Florida, Loretta tried her best to interest her in a half dozen other properties. But none of them stood out for her client. So in a last-ditch effort, she caved in and decided to show her the mini mansion on Hawk's Bend.

As Loretta pulled into the drive, Christine gasped. "It's gorgeous!'

Loretta was afraid that she would react that way. The same way the Magrews reacted when they first saw the property.

"It was built about ten years ago," she told her. "Has every convenience and enough land to herd cattle."

They stopped in front of the portico and Christine jumped out to fully appreciate what she was seeing. "Looks like a modern Tara from *Gone with the Wind*."

"A lot of people say that," Loretta said through the open car window. She remained inside the vehicle to give Christine a chance to examine the front of the house, she watched her take out her cell phone and begin snapping pictures.

Loretta adjusted her black-framed eyeglasses and peered up at the house. For some reason, it gave her the willies. Maybe it was the isolation? She couldn't say. It just felt creepy.

Late one night, when everyone is asleep, a dark figure with horrible intentions breaks in through an unlocked door. With axe in hand, he quietly skulks through the house, creeping to the rooms upstairs. Then without warning, with psychotic precision, he brings the blade down onto the head of every adult, every child. Skull bones shatter, brains ooze, blood splatters. No one knew what hit them, no one had a chance. Dragging his blood-soaked axe behind him, he calmly descends the staircase, disappearing into the night, leaving nothing alive, except, a potted plant.

Loretta shivered. "God, I gotta stop watching so many horror movies," she told herself.

"I love the fountain," Christine said, interrupting Loretta's nightmarish daydream. Loretta shook off the thoughts, emerged from the car to join her on the portico.

"My husband will love the big garage. Three cars!" she said, taking a photo of the parking area.

Loretta waited patiently until Christine had absorbed the surroundings, took more pictures, and was ready to step inside.

"You ain't seen nothin' yet," she said, sounding more like a carnival hawker than a real estate agent.

They entered the marbled foyer, with gilded mirrors, and huge windows reaching up to the second floor. Christine, spun around, snapping more photos. Lifting her eyes, she gazed in wonderment at the sparkling chandelier suspended above their heads, disbelieving that this might be their new home.

By now, the Magrews had had all their furniture, kitchenware, pictures, every remnant of their prior inhabitance removed. As a result, the house appeared more massive, more desolate, and colder than it had when it was occupied. Loretta's comfort level wasn't getting any better. She hoped Christine would not ask why the former owners moved out. But in truth, she really didn't know. They told her nothing. Maybe it had been marital discord, maybe a family emergency. Regardless, if the question were to be posed, she could honestly plead ignorance.

"Very different than what we'd be moving from," Christine said, breaking into Loretta's thoughts. "We have an eighteenth-century gem. I really love it, but my husband got a position he couldn't say no to."

Loretta just let Christine wander around, room to room, snapping more shots, pausing now and then in an attempt to take in everything. She exhibited the same exuberance that Jessie and Peter demonstrated on their showing. Her hope was that Christine would find the place "not her style." Face it, from a small charming 1700s home to a twenty-first-century behemoth, it could be overwhelming. But Loretta kept her feelings to herself. She liked Christine. She seemed down to earth, the kid-friendly schoolteacher type, which is what she said she did back up in New York. There was no flash to her, not like some of these well-to-do Florida divas with their expensive bangles and designer couture, rushing off to their Pilates classes or their doctors for a shot of Botox. Christine was quite the opposite. She wore a conservative Laura Ashley-ish flowered skirt, simple open-toed sandals, a watch, a necklace, and two rings—her engagement diamond and a simple gold wedding band. Not that her hips couldn't use a few sessions of spinning or her hair an updated redo. Loretta berated herself. She could use a little help too. Who was she to be critical? Bottom line: Christine, and she could only assume, her entire family, were grounded and real. It was refreshing.

Christine was drawn to the family room. She hesitated at the floor-to-ceiling windows to peer out upon the property, she took another photo, then slid open a nearby glass door and stepped out onto the patio.

Loretta followed behind, poised to answer any questions.

Christine, stood as if hypnotized, gazing upon the land that spread out in all directions. Her attention was particularly focused on the barrier of palms and shrubs. She had a sudden and inexplicable sensation of belonging. That she was supposed to be here. A passing flock of ibis fluttering overhead caught her eye. They veered, swooped above the land, then disappeared over the palm trees, disappearing from sight.

Curiously, Loretta studied her blank expression, then broke the trance to point out the building at their left. "That's the pool house. Shower, toilet." Then she pointed out the barbeque and the bar, also topped with the same gorgeous granite that was used for the kitchen counters inside. But she wasn't certain if Christine was listening.

Then she spoke: "This beats being up north. Sometimes we get snow up to the windowsills."

"No fear of that here," Loretta said, deciding to ignore Christine's peculiar behavior.

"By the way, those thickets," she said, pointing, her arm sweeping in an arc, the same thickets where the birds flew. "It encloses all of the land and is the property boundary on all sides. Nothing but swamp behind."

Christine's shielded her eyes from the sun with her hand and focused again on the unmanicured wall of scrub and cabbage palm. More photos.

"I love gardening," she said, ignoring what Loretta had just said. "I can see all sorts of fruit trees, flower beds. I'll be a terribly busy lady."

She raised the phone to take additional shots. "I want to show my husband everything."

"Of course," Loretta said, understanding. "Oh," she added, somewhat abruptly. "Be careful. There are gators back there."

Christine spun around. With a glint of fear, she gasped. "Seriously?" Now understanding why Loretta mentioned it.

"You're in Florida. They're everywhere. Just use a little caution and you'll be fine." She didn't know why she felt compelled to say anything about alligators. It just came out. Yet, if it dissuaded her from wanting the place, it might be a good thing.

With a sudden change in her mood, Christine reconsidered. "Actually, that's kinda cool. My eleven-year-old son will love the nature angle. He's a bit of a smarty and gets hooked on one thing after another. Last month, it was everything about the American Southwest. He read about the tribes, the pueblos, the history. And the month before that, he was on a nautical kick. If you ever want to know anything about eighteenth-century schooners to modern cruise ships, he'll have the answer. At least he's using his mind and reading a lot."

"You also mentioned a daughter?"

Christine released an audible sigh. "Maggie. She's thirteen. I think this move will be hardest on her." Christine thought a moment about her, attempting to see her in this environment. "She's at *that* time of her life. She needs her circle of friends, always on the go. You know how teenage girls can be."

Loretta nodded. She had once been one. Nothing but boys, clothes, and gossip filling their heads.

"Michael, my son, will love it, though. She really has no choice. We *are* moving to South Florida."

Loretta motioned for her to follow. They returned to the foyer, to the bottom step, to a staircase so grand that Christine could almost imagine royalty descending from their palatial boudoirs above. As they climbed, Christine let her hand caress the solid oak railing, enjoying the coolness of the wood.

Once upstairs, Loretta gave Christine the freedom to explore on her own. "There are four bedrooms and a master, a full bath for each room. Walk-in closets."

Christine paused to decide where to start. "At that end?" pointing, she indicated the last room on the left.

"That's the master," Loretta said. "It's got a great view of the back. You can even get a glimpse of the swamp."

But Christine wandered down the hall in the opposite direction, toward the other bedrooms. Loretta would wait, and leaned up against the railing to peer down to the foyer below. The atmosphere inside the house seemed so dark and heavy. In spite of the many windows, hardly any sunlight got through. *Maybe they're just in need of a good cleaning,* she thought. Nevertheless, it was a little unnerving, and she wondered if Christine also noticed.

Christine saved the master until the last. She had begun her tour at the opposite end of the hall, investigating the three additional bedrooms, all of ample size, all with walk-in closets, all with their own bathrooms. *The kids will love it*, she thought.

Inside the master, she stopped to gape at the enormity of the room, twice the size of any of the other rooms. The vastness of the his-and-her bathrooms caused her head to spin. As Loretta had indicated, there was a walk-in closet, one for her, another for her husband, Stan. Closets neither could ever fill. Floor-to-ceiling windows that, indeed, provided an optimal view out onto the pool and the lawns, as well as those swamps. She aimed her camera toward the lawns and the palms beyond snapping more photos. In one, she managed to catch that flock of ibis rising above the trees and once again disappearing back into the swamp.

"It's a dream house," Christine gushed.

Finally, when she seemed to have seen enough, she returned to Loretta's side, and together, they descended the staircase to the front door. But before they left the building Christine asked, "Okay. Give me the bad news. What are they asking? This really can't be in our price range."

Loretta paused a moment and slowly nodded, "Yeah, it is."

"What?" Christine gasped.

Loretta told her the price.

"Impossible!" Christine said.

Loretta shook her head. "That's the price."

"My God! It would be like stealing."

"If you're not interested in committing a crime," Loretta said, breaking into a smile, "I can show you something else."

"No! No!" Christine insisted. "Let me discuss this with my husband and I'll call you. Tomorrow. In the morning."

Together, they returned to the car and Loretta turned the key. "I'm in the office at nine. You have my personal number. You can call me anytime."

Christine gazed out at all the palms and flowering trees that grew along the roadside. Everything was so Florida—so tropical, so colorful, so perfect. Her mind was spinning with excitement and anticipation. Unless Stan had some solid objections, Hawk's Bend is going to be their new home. That she was convinced. Then oddly, she had the strange sensation, as she had had earlier, that it was calling out to her. That she was chosen to live there. But that was ridiculous. She brushed off the notion, and instead imagined how wonderful their new life will be.

*****

Loretta pulled into the parking lot of her real estate office and parked next to Christine's rental car.

Christine turned to face Loretta. "Thank you so much!" She stepped out of the car, gave Loretta a wave goodbye, and returned to her own vehicle.

Loretta, waved goodbye back and stepped out of her car and into the office.

Neville, coworker, sat at his desk entering data into his computer. He paused when he spotted Loretta. "How did it go?" he asked.

"I guess okay. She was interested," she replied.

Loretta went to her desk to check for any phone messages, then after noting down a few numbers which she decided to return the next morning, she decided to call it a day.

On the drive home, a gnawing feeling came over her. She truly hoped that Christine and her husband would pass and decide on something else. There was no rational reason why she thought that. She was a real estate agent, after all. She wanted to make sales, not dissuade a client from purchasing a property. Yet she wished they would pass. But why would they? Or anyone? The Magrews came to mind. They jumped on it as soon as they saw it, but she reminded herself, they jumped out of it just four months later.

"Listen, sweetie," Loretta said to her husband upon entering her house. She tried to remain calm as she saw her husband still watching television. It's where she left him when she went to work that morning. "I'm working my butt off trying to make ends meet while you work to make a permanent indentation of your butt in that chair."

Her husband of twenty-five years, Matty, ignored her comment.

"Did you tell them?" he asked instead.

"Tell them what?" She crossed her arms against her chest as if to protect herself from whatever he was going to say.

"About all the other owners who bailed so mysteriously." His eyes remained focused on the television.

She stepped in the space between Matty and the television, took a deep breath, and began: "The fact is, I don't know why all the previous owners moved out so unexpectedly and so soon after they had moved in. There were no reasons given. So there's nothing to withhold. And if it were unhappy marriages or a death in the family, it would be none of my business anyway." She started to step back to the kitchen but paused. "In fact, I wasn't thrilled at showing that place today, but if they buy, then there'll be a commission. And by God, we can use it!"

Matty sighed. "You know about that place?"

"Know what?" Loretta asked.

"Come on," he returned. "Everyone knows."

"I repeat, know what?"

"It's haunted!"

"Oh, please. Are you watching those ghost programs again? It's nothing of the sort."

"I know guys who have driven out there at night. They hear weird sounds. See lights flicker inside the house. A bunch of things."

"Well, those guys were probably too drunk to experience anything real. Car lights reflect off windows, and there's lots of sounds that come out of the swamp…gators, frogs…" She couldn't continue with this conversation and told Matty so.

He settled back in the chair and sipped his beer. "Fine with me if you don't believe it, but I ain't never stepping foot in that place—ever!"

"Well, unless you want to buy it, you won't have to," Loretta said from the kitchen. She pulled the makings for salad from the bottom refrigerator drawers and began to chop.

CHAPTER 3

Christine pulled her car beneath the porte-cochere where a valet dressed in a neat blue jacket with gold shoulder epaulettes, greeted her, welcoming her back to the hotel. He kindly escorted her into the lobby.

"Have a wonderful evening, Mrs. Minter," he said.

She smiled at the over the top luxury and friendliness of the Le Soleil Hotel and Resort but for what they charged and the worldwide reputation the chain had, it had to be over the top.

"Mrs. Minter! So nice to see you," Jeff the bellman said.

She accepted his hand and shook cordially.

"We're looking forward to working for Mr. Minter. Everyone loves him!"

Christine smiled again. *They should love him*, she thought. *He is not only a terrific husband and father, but an excellent hotel manager.*

"That's so good to hear, Jeff." Then she asked, "Do you know where Mr. Minter is right now?"

He put up his finger, indicating that he'd be right back, hurried to the front desk and said something to the agent behind the counter.

"He's in meetings right now," he told her upon his return. "Would you like me to call him out?"

"Oh no!" she said. "No, not at all." She headed for the bank of elevators. "I'll be in the room."

Jeff gave a little salute and a bow from the waist as she disappeared.

After she settled into their posh suite of rooms otherwise known as the fifteenth-story penthouse, she took out her cell and dialed home.

"Hey," she said when she heard her mother's voice. "Yes, everything is going fabulously. Mom, this hotel is incredible. I think Stan will do a wonderful job. And I think I found a house, but I have to discuss it with Stan first." Christine tried to quell her excitement but was having little success.

"How are the kids?" She listened to the update: Maggie's anticipation of the upcoming summer break, Michael's nose pressed into books, or eyes glued to the television to watch the Discovery Channel and National Geographic, nothing unusual for him.

"And you are doing okay, Mom?" She listened to her mother relate all the goings-on in the neighborhood and whatever else she could think of telling.

"Good, good. Okay, listen, as soon as I have details about the house and getting everything moved down here, I'll call. Oh, you're gonna love visiting down her, Mom. Love you and give my love to the kids."

She plugged the cell into the phone charger and grabbed a bottle of water from the minibar. Then she slid aside the doors and took a seat on the spacious sun-filled balcony.

What a view, she thought, marveling at the expanse of the blue gulf waters stretching out before her, sparkling as if millions of diamonds were dancing across its surface. To the north was the city of Naples, a city she had yet to explore. All she was aware of was that many a millionaire-owned homes there. To the south was Marco Island, another playground for the rich and a popular vacation destination for many a traveler. Her attention was suddenly drawn to a pair of dolphins, leisurely cruising south along the beach. As much as she adored living in western New York, she couldn't deny that she was now in paradise.

How fortunate. Her husband would be overseeing the operation of the two most elegant, five-star hotels of South Florida—well, at least until they find a general manager for the Palm Beach property. Then this alone would be the home base for Stan. She looked up at the clear heavens, "Thank you, Lord, for all our fortune. It is so appreciated."

The jingling of the hotel phone broke her reverie. It was Stan.

"Hi, honey," she said. "No problem. Whenever you're finished, I'll be in the room. Oh, I think I found the perfect house!" Her exhilaration was growing. "I have photos of everything. Later, you'll be able to view them, and you can give me your opinion. Yes, I know you trust me and my taste in things, but I really want you to share this with me. It is a major step."

He said something that gave her a nice warm feeling, and she smiled. "Love you too. See you later."

*****

Christine was luxuriating in the oversized bathtub, the warm water scented with the lavender bath salts supplied by the hotel. Her imaginings took her back to that beautiful house. She could see each room, every step of that majestic staircase, even the grand, sweeping views of the landscape. She was lost in her thoughts of how their life would soon be. But her thoughts were suddenly interrupted by the slamming room door and Stan calling out to her.

"Sorry I'm so late," she heard as he apologized from behind the closed bathroom door.

Excitedly, she jumped out of the water, dried herself off, and pulled on the thick, plush robe that was offered in every room.

"What time is it?" she asked as she embraced him.

"Almost seven."

It was later than she thought, but no matter. No dinner to fix, no homework assignments to supervise, no laundry. Just the two of them. Opening the minibar, she pulled out a miniature of vodka and emptied it into an ice-filled glass. Handing it to her husband, she then poured herself a glass of white wine and proceeded to retrieve her phone.

"All right!" he said with his free hand in the air as if giving up. "You won't relax until I look at the pictures, right?"

She smiled back. "That's right. You know me, when I get a bug up my butt, I won't quit." She opened the photo gallery app on her phone, went to the first shot, which was the pineapple-capped water feature, handed him the phone and said, "Just scroll."

Still in his suit jacket and tie, he sat on the edge of the bed and began to slowly swipe his fingertip across the screen.

"Wow!" he said more than once. "The place is huge!"

Christine nodded and waited, hoping he would be as excited as she was. "A wine cellar?"

"It's called a closet, I think," Christine clarified.

After a minute, he stopped scrolling and asked, "Who's that?"

Christine leaned over his shoulder to peer at the small screen. "Who's who?"

It was one of the photos she took of the back property. He pointed to something standing among the thickets. "It looks like a man."

She leaned in closer. It did look like a man!

The next photo showed another figure, this one on the lawn, outside the shadow of the trees. It was also a man; they could clearly make him out. Two men had been out there.

"I didn't see anybody when I took the shots."

"They seemed to have been staring right at you."

A little shiver ran down her spine. "It must have been a play of sunlight," she concluded. "It has to be!"

He was coming to the last pictures.

"Well, what do you think?" Her impatience was tangible.

He rattled the ice in the glass and asked her what the price was.

When she told him, the ice stopped rattling. "Seriously?"

She nodded. "I know. It seems too good to be true."

Her husband returned the phone and leaned back against the bed pillows, rapt in thought. "Do you love it?" he finally asked.

"It's as if it were calling to me," she said. She thought for a moment to what she had just said. But it *was* true. She now realized, that in an odd and unconscious way, the house was calling to her, enticing her, luring her to take ownership.

"Do you think the kids will like it?"

"Michael will love anything we buy. Maggie will be miserable no matter what. She just doesn't want to move. What's more," she remembered as a selling point, "it is just twenty minutes to the hotel.

No major roads so no traffic jams. It's not far from a grocery store and I'm told the schools are good, and they're not far either."

"You know I trust you and whatever you want is fine with me. There's too much for me to do around here so I won't get any time to see it myself. Maybe a glimpse at some point. So…" he paused and reached up for her hand. "Call the agent in the morning and make an offer…contingent on the sale of our place."

Christine could have leapt into his lap from the excitement. Instead, she gently leaned in and kissed him. She caught her breath. "Okay. Here's the plan," she began. "I'll fly home and get everything started. When the kids are finished with school—that's only a few weeks away—and the house is packed, and the movers are ready to go…and we have an offer on our house, We'll hop on a flight home—our new home." She liked the way that sounded: their new home.

He smiled one of those smiles that captured her heart years earlier and shook his head. "Mrs. Organized. You have everything worked out. I love you and think this will be a great adventure."

Christine put her glass of wine down and placed her arms upon her hips. "Okay, Mr. Organized. Get changed and we'll go celebrate."

The next morning, as her husband showered, she dialed Loretta's number.

"Hi, Loretta. It's Christine Minter. My husband and I spoke, and we want to make an offer."

Loretta hesitated before responding. The dreaded moment had arrived.

Chapter 4

On exactly the last day of school, the Minter's New York home sold—and at a better price than they could ever expect. The moving van loaded up the last carton and piece of furniture and began its journey to Florida. The hotel was paying for the move, and it was where they would stay until everything had been delivered to the house. Events were moving fast and too smoothly. But who was she to question such good fortune?

The time of reckoning finally arrived. They piled into Christine's mother's car and started for the airport.

"My life is over," Maggie moaned as she watched the only life she had known slip away.

"Come on, sweetie," Christine consoled. "It's the beginning of an adventure. You'll meet lots of new friends. You'll have the beach all year round."

"Beach?" Maggie asked, her mood brightening.

"Yes. Didn't I mention that earlier? We'll be in easy access to the beach." She watched her daughter in the rearview mirror, happy that she might have hit a nerve. Hoping to add more icing on the cake, she informed them that the house has a swimming pool and there were acres of land.

"At the far end," she added, more for her son's benefit, "there's a swamp, part of the Everglades, way out back, and that means alligators."

Michael's mouth dropped. "Really? That is so cool." He reached into the canvas bag he brought. It was stuffed with books. He selected one and held it up so Christine could see it. *The History of Florida* she read.

"Mom, there used to be a lot of pirate ships around Florida. There's a museum in Key West with a ton of booty on display. Can we go there sometime?"

"Of course," she said, glad to have someone else sharing her enthusiasm.

Once at the airport, Grandma hugged the kids and then her daughter. "Have a safe trip and make certain you call me when you get there."

Some hours later, they were soaring among the clouds, heading for Naples.

"We'll get you two enrolled in a new school right away. I want us to get settled as soon as we can, so we can enjoy our new life, new adventures."

Maggie stared idly out the small oval window, ear buds inserted, isolated from chatter, watching the world fade away. But Michael beamed. He had never flown before. The experience was exhilarating.

"It's like being an explorer," he said.

"Yes, it is," Christine agreed.

"How long will it take us to get there?" Michael asked.

"Not too long, just a few more hours."

CHAPTER 5

The only disappointment Christine had was that their furniture from their New York home created not only a sparseness due to the size of the rooms, but it was wrong for the modern eclectic décor. Nevertheless, as she moved through the house, making mental notes, she was elated that the initial move was over. Their former house had sold for an unexpected windfall profit, her husband was making more money, and the summer had just begun so the kids would have some free time to get acquainted to their new environs. Everything was going so smoothly. As she descended the staircase, the doorbell chimed. It was the first time she had heard it since no one had ever come by. She was surprised to see Loretta.

"Hope I'm not interrupting anything," she stated.

"Absolutely not!" Christine said, thrilled to have her first visitor. "Please come in."

Loretta proffered a basket of wine and cheese, crackers, and small bags of assorted goodies. "I thought a housewarming gift was fitting."

"You didn't have to do that!" Christine said. Nevertheless, she took the basket from Loretta and motioned for her to follow.

"Let me show you around." She paused. "But first, a glass of wine to toast. You do like wine?"

"Absolutely!"

Loretta followed Christine into the kitchen, noticing the fresh touches that had been made.

"Our stuff really doesn't go well with the house, but we'll get around to doing some interior designing down the road," Christine said as she poured two glasses of chardonnay. "Come out back and meet the kids."

They stepped out into the Florida heat. Maggie was lounging in a chaise, lost in whatever was playing through her headphones, and Michael was splashing around in the water.

"Hey, kids!" Christine called out. Michael immediately swam to the pool's edge closest to his mom. But Maggie heard nothing.

Noticing, Michael slapped water and sent a spray across his sister's face.

Maggie screamed then saw her mother.

"Kids, this is Loretta. She is the real estate agent who sold us the house."

Loretta gave a little wave.

"This place is so awesome," Michael cried out. "I love it."

Loretta looked over at Maggie who was putting earbuds back in. "It's okay. Kinda in the middle of nowhere," she said, with little enthusiasm.

Christine shot an apologetic glance at Loretta. "Remember what I told you when I came to look at the place. Nothing makes her happy."

They returned inside to where it was cooler and sat at the kitchen table.

"This heat and humidity will take some getting used to," Christine said.

"Pretty soon, you won't even notice," Loretta said. "So has everything been all right with the house?"

Curiously, Christine tilted her head. "In what way?"

Loretta feared she may have opened a can of worms, worms that she didn't believe, although her husband and his pals did. "I mean, is the air conditioner working, the electricity, the water—those kinds of things?"

"Oh! Yes! Everything is great. We just got satellite TV installed yesterday." She paused to think. "Well, the lights have flickered from time to time, but I guess it's just local connections or who knows. Nothing to be concerned about."

"So you said you loved to garden," Loretta said, changing the subject. "What will you plant? There's so much land."

"Well, I'm thinking fruit trees at first. We had a couple apple trees back home, but here, I can put in oranges, lemons, an avocado tree although I'd probably be the only one who would eat them."

"There's a fabulous garden store down on Weatherly. It's the best of its kind around here," Loretta said. "They'll give you great advice and ideas. They'll even come out and test the soil and deliver whatever you need."

Just then a loud thump sounded above their heads. Loretta fell silent, and they both looked toward the ceiling. Christine shrugged it off as nothing more than a beam or a wall support shifting. Their old house made all kinds of sounds.

Loretta set her empty wineglass down, and Christine refilled it.

"Let me ask," Christine began tentatively. "Who originally built this place and why so secluded, surrounded by all this property?"

Loretta thought for a moment. "I don't know the whole story, but a couple came out here about twelve years ago. They were from Germany and had a lot of money. They bought all these acres and then built the house. Took two years to complete construction. From the records, they only lived here for maybe three years, then they packed up and left. Back to Germany? No one knows."

"So who lived here afterward?"

Loretta feared these questions might arise. But like she told her husband, she could only relate what she knew. "A family of five moved in after the Germans left. They stayed here for about six months and then they put it up for sale. Then it sat empty for quite a while until the Magrews moved in. The people you bought it from."

"And how long did they stay?"

Loretta breathed in, then let the air out slowly. "Only four months."

"That's so odd," Christine said. "Any reasons why people didn't stay long here?"

Loretta shook her head. "I frankly don't know. My only speculations are that there was marital discourse, family emergencies, or maybe it was just so out of the way that every errand became a full day's job."

"But there are stores less than twenty minutes from here," Christine reminded her.

"Yes, but those places opened up within the last four or five years. Otherwise, you'd have to drive at least forty-five minutes to grocery shop."

Christine thought about the logic of it, that those conveniences were here even when the former owners were here. Her thoughts were interrupted by a scream emanating from outside.

They both jumped from the table and rushed poolside to see Maggie and Michael huddled on the chaise.

"What is it?" Christine shrieked, fearing that one of them had drowned though they were both safely on dry land.

Maggie pointed down to the end of the yard, to the brambles and sabal palms.

"A man!" Maggie said.

Both women redirected their attention to where the lawn ended.

"Where?" Christine asked. "Michael, did you see anyone?"

"No, Ma. Maggie is just being a drama queen."

Christine wondered where he had heard that before but was interrupted by Maggie.

"Mom, I saw him. Standing down on the right."

"What did he look like?" Loretta asked.

"He was dark-skinned. He wasn't wearing a shirt either."

From her frightened demeanor, Christine knew that Maggie believed she saw someone. "Maybe it was just a play of shadows,'" she suggested.

"*No*! There was a man."

"Well, whoever it was, he's gone now," Christine said, trying to bring some calm.

Loretta spoke up, "You know, here in Florida, it's not unusual for people to go swamping—you know, they slog their way through the muck. Sort of a backwoods hobby. Mucking."

Maggie's face twisted up. "Why would anyone want to go into that place? That's just plain messed up."

"I think so too," Loretta agreed. "But this is the South. People do things a little differently down here. But getting to my point, you may have just seen someone going through the swamp looking for gators or frogs. I don't think it's anything to worry about."

Christine could see her daughter beginning to relax. The ladies returned to the kitchen and resumed drinking their wine.

"Thank you." She sighed.

"For what?" Loretta asked.

"For a little rational thinking. I think that really put her at ease."

"Oh, it is the truth," Loretta insisted. "Some old traditions die hard. Especially when you start talking about the people who live out there."

"People really do live out there?" Christine asked, both surprised and appalled.

"Absolutely! Throughout the state, there are indigenous people and just plain swamp folk whose families have been out there for hundreds of years. Of course, now the Indians make a fortune with the gambling, but that's another story." Loretta let out a little laugh.

Christine laughed too, and it felt good. She had been so concerned about setting up the house, accommodating her kids, and running errands, that she seemed to have lost her sense of humor.

"Thank you. I needed a light moment." She reached for the remaining wine and emptied the bottle into their glasses. "Do you have family?" she asked.

Loretta nodded, feeling now the euphoric effects of her drink. "Oh yeah! I have a daughter out in California. She's a good kid. Almost twenty-two and happily pursuing a career in oceanography. Don't know why she couldn't do it here considering we're surrounded by the sea. Then I've got a deadbeat husband..."

Christine raised an eyebrow.

"Okay, maybe that's a little harsh. He used to be a bank manager, but they had cutbacks, and he was let go. That was two months ago. Meanwhile, he sits his lazy ass in a chair all day watching what I call Stupid TV, collects unemployment, and hasn't even looked for a job."

"'Lazy ass'?" Christine repeated, breaking into a wine-induced smile. "It's just funny hearing you use that term."

Loretta took another sip. "How did you and Stan meet?"

Christine became a little misty, remembering the first time they met. "I was a waitress in a restaurant. You know, one of these national chains serving up burgers and brew. Stan was hired as manager. I was trying to make some money and finish school. All I ever wanted was to be a teacher. But anyway, Stan and I hit it off. He was tall and handsome with the most gorgeous black hair and blue eyes. We began to secretly see each other."

"Secretly?" Loretta asked.

"Yeah, it was a company policy that you couldn't date coworkers. Understandable. And neither one of us could quit, so we met for dinners and hoped we wouldn't run into anyone from work."

"Does Stan have family?"

"No. Nobody. He was adopted by a couple who couldn't have kids, but they both passed. I think his father, who I never met, died of cancer, and his mom died in a car accident. It was pretty tragic. I think that's why he puts so much importance on our family. Like the one he never had."

Loretta smiled. "Well, he's got a beautiful family."

"Thanks," Christine replied.

Loretta glanced at her watch. "I hate to end this wine fest, but I have a showing this afternoon…and I'm not looking forward to it, except if they buy. All they want to see are mega million-dollar palaces on the beach, which is fine. But what a couple of snoots."

Christine escorted Loretta to the door. "I've really enjoyed this visit. I hope we can do lunch or have you and the lazy-ass over for dinner."

They both laughed again.

"I hope we can be friends," Christine said.

"We already are," Loretta assured her. "And call me for anything. Interior designer, you mentioned earlier. I know a great one and he won't rob you. Check out that garden shop I mentioned and enjoy the basket. Oh, and I look forward to seeing your husband again. I knew right away, when you came for the closing, he was no lazy ass!"

They both laughed again, then Christine stood on the portico, dwarfed by the imposing pillars, watching Loretta's car circle around the fountain and disappear down the drive.

*****

By the time Stan returned home, Christine had already set the table, lit the outdoor grill, and taken steaks from the refrigerator.

He poured himself a drink and wandered outside to see the kids. Michael, by now, was in a chair his head deep into the pages of a book, and Maggie was texting friends back in New York. But when they saw Stan, they both squealed, jumped from their seats, ran across the pool deck to bear hugs.

"Well, how has your day been, guys?"

Michael, positive as ever, smiled and said he had been in the pool all day. Maggie, though, returned to her seat with a frown. "Not much to do around here. And it's hot, and there were people watching us from down there." She pointed to the brambles.

"What do you mean, people"? Stan inquired.

Christine, now at the grill, flames sizzling the meat, kept an ear to their conversation.

"Some guy with dark skin and no shirt just stood there, looking up at us. Then he just disappeared."

Stan turned to Michael. "Did you see him?"

Michael shook his head. "Maggie's just bored."

Christine left the steaks to grill a few more minutes and joined Stan.

"Well, how was your day?" he asked.

"Actually, pretty good. Loretta stopped by, and we chatted. I think we'll be good friends. We both heard Maggie scream."

This caught Stan's attention. His daughter may not be the most enthusiastic of kids, but she would never lie or make something up. "Did you see anyone?" he asked.

Christine shook her head. "But," she added, hesitating for a moment, "how she described him sounded like that guy who showed up in the photos I took."

Now Stan was concerned. Concerned about the safety of his family and their new home. But he decided to keep it to himself and speak to Christine later, when the kids had gone to bed.

"As for me," he said, rattling his glass indicating that it was empty. Christine ran inside for more vodka. When she returned, he continued. "I had one hell of a day. Everyone wants to run the show their way, and some of them have some good ideas."

"Such as?" Christine asked.

"Such as, every month I gather a representative from every department and have a little pow-wow. Listen to their concerns, their problems, how things can improve. Other hotels—and businesses— do it. I'm surprised they haven't already implemented it."

Maggie continued to text, showing little interest in her father's chatter. Her apathy did not go unnoticed.

"I also made a decision that since it's summer break, we're going to have a party!" Stan announced in a raised voice.

Maggie tilted her head slightly. Michael was all ears.

"I'm going to invite all the department managers and their immediate families to the house, and we'll barbeque hamburgers, hot dogs, chicken. They can swim, sun, whatever." Stan waited a moment for a response. Then he added, "You'll meet some new kids. There will be a lot of them the same ages as you."

Michael caught on. "Yeah, Dad. That will be so awesome."

Maggie finally looked up from her texting. "Yeah, Dad, that might be fun." She looked back at her phone, wondering if she spelled *dismal* correctly, then wrote *bored* in all caps.

Christine checked the steaks, announced that they were ready and called everyone inside to the kitchen table. There was bread and salad—a very casual dinner, but one she knew her family enjoyed.

"What was that?" Maggie suddenly blurted.

"What was what?" Christine asked.

"Sounds like someone's walking upstairs."

"I heard it too" Michael concurred.

They stopped eating and Stan stood up. "There's no one upstairs." Nevertheless, he grabbed his steak knife and proceeded to the foyer, peering up the staircase. He decided that if he came this far, he may as well go up and look. After few minutes, he reemerged into the kitchen announcing that nobody was there, and it had to be the wind or the house settling. "Remember our house in New York. There was always a creak or a groan."

"But this house isn't that old," Maggie said.

"I know. The more the reason that it's just settling," he said. "Now let's eat."

When everything was finished—including the chocolate cake Christine had purchased in the bakery section of the grocery store—and the table cleared, Stan and Christine sent the kids to their rooms to watch the new satellite television just installed.

Stan motioned for Christine to follow him back to the patio. Where they both sat and gazed at the incredibly clear night sky. Stars spangled the blackness and from the swamp beyond, frogs croaked in a musical chorus.

"Man, it gets hot here in the summer," Stan sighed.

"And the mosquitos," Christine added, swatting at a few above their heads.

Then Stan got serious. "You know this talk about guys watching you from down there concerns me."

"Oh, come on. Loretta told me how people like to go swamping or mucking or whatever it's called through all that mud and mire trying to catch alligators and those frogs. I'm sure it's just some harmless locals."

"Still," he added. "I think we should put in a security system, maybe cameras. I'm surprised one isn't already installed. Maybe," he added, carefully. "I should get a gun."

"Oh no! I don't want something like that in this house!" Her head was shaking back and forth. "I'm adamantly opposed to that idea!"

Stan got quiet. He knew his wife. Sometimes you just had to back off until another time. "By the way, have you seen my watch? I always put it on the night table, but this morning, it was gone."

Christine shrugged. "You must have misplaced it somewhere."

"Probably," Stan replied.

"Maybe tomorrow, I could bring the kids to the hotel for lunch and then take Maggie out for a little shopping or sightseeing. She's in need of some personal attention. Michael can hang by the pool with his books for few hours. He'll be fine."

"Sounds perfect!" Stan agreed.

"And when do you want to have this pool party?" she asked.

"Maybe in a month. On a Saturday or Sunday. The hotel will still be open, so some people will have a hard time adjusting schedules. And I'll have to take some time to get up to Palm Beach, to look at that property. I'm sure they'll find a new GM soon. This is going to be a well-paid but busy position. You may not see a lot of me, until I can get a solid footing on everything," he said, preparing her for future dinners without him at the table.

"No worries, honey. We'll adjust, and there's still a lot of things I need to do here. I hate how the furniture looks in this place, and I want to start my gardening. Loretta told me of a great place for everything I might need."

Stan leaned over and placed a kiss on her cheek. "That's one of the many reasons I love you. You're independent and low maintenance."

She smiled wryly. "Wait to you get the bills for Maggie's shopping spree and new furniture. Not to mention all my gardening implements."

A scream came from upstairs. They jumped from their seats and raced up the stairs. It came from Maggie's room. Michael was already there, sitting on the bed next to his trembling sister.

"What is it?" Christine shrieked.

It took few a moment for her daughter to compose herself. She pointed to the closet.

Stan and Christine exchanged quizzical glances.

"There's somebody in there. He looked like that man I saw before."

Stan bravely approached the closet door, grabbed the handle, and pulled it wide open. Nothing. Nothing except her clothes hanging neatly from the rod, her shoes below and a few other items on the shelf up top. Stan said nothing. He stepped aside, so his daughter could get a clear view.

"But there *was* someone there! He pushed the door open and stepped toward me. When I screamed, he went back in." Tears began to stain her cheeks.

Christine sat next to her and put her arm around her shoulders. "Okay, okay, but no one is there now. Do you want to sleep in our room tonight?"

Maggie wasn't about to lose all her pride. "No, Mom, I'm not sharing a room with my parents. That would be too…weird."

"Listen. Tomorrow, I'm taking the two of you for lunch at the hotel—or any other place you want. I'm leaving Michael at the hotel's pool, and I'm taking you for a shopping spree. How does that sound?"

Suddenly, Maggie wasn't thinking about strangers in her room and began to beam. "Really?" Christine's suggestion seemed to alleviate Maggie's trembling.

"Yes, really. We'll leave about eleven so both of you be ready. Michael bring your books or whatever—"

Michael cut her off. "How come she gets to go shopping and I don't?"

Christine peered into his clenched face, his lips pouty, noticing a little anger. This was a reaction and an expression very unusual for her son. "Because, you will get your turn later."

He was appeased, his features adjusted back to their happy positions.

"It's late. Let's get some sleep." She addressed her daughter. "Leave the lights on."

"I am," Maggie quietly replied.

They gave the kids goodnight kisses, followed Michael to his room, making sure he was all right and then headed back to the kitchen. Christine poured a little more wine and Stan more vodka. They didn't realize until now, how shaken up they were.

"She was dreaming," Christine suggested. "She had that guy she allegedly saw earlier in her mind, and he became part of a dream. That's all."

"Sounds rational to me." Stan agreed. "But I'm still going to consider that security system."

They finished their drinks, proceeded to one room then the next, making certain that all the doors and windows were locked. Afterward, they climbed the stairs and went to bed.

CHAPTER 6

The next morning, on their ride to the hotel, Maggie put down her phone. "Mom?"

Christine looked into the rearview. "Yes, honey?"

"I don't like the house," she stated bluntly.

"Actually," Christine remarked. "We didn't think you would."

This seemed to surprise her. "Really? Why?"

"Honey," Christine began carefully. "We love you to death. But it can be difficult to please you."

"Yeah!" Michael blurted.

"Stay out of this, Michael." Christine placed her hand gently on his knee and gave it a little squeeze.

"But it's true!" the girl said. "It's got a strange feeling to it."

Maggie, peeved, peered out the window quietly pondering the passing palm trees and empty fields until houses began to appear, building into communities. Then she spoke. "Don't you notice how gloomy it is? It's like a cloud has settled in all the rooms."

"No," Christine replied tersely. "And if it is, then we'll get someone in to wash all the windows."

No one spoke again until they reached the hotel. "Let's go have some lunch. I'm starving," Christine said as they were met with the familiar flourish of smiling valets and welcoming bellman. Many employees greeted the kids especially. They had spent several days in the penthouse giving a chance for the staff to acquaint themselves with their new boss' family, familiarizing themselves to their names, their likes, dislikes.

Choosing a table on the patio, she ordered chicken fingers for the kids and a burger for herself as they admired the beautiful shimmering Gulf.

"Isn't this prettier than New York?" Christine asked.

"It's different," Maggie mumbled glumly.

"C'mon, Maggie!" Michael said. "No more snow. There's the beach. And we have a swimming pool!"

Christine sipped on her mimosa and studied her two children as they ate. She loved them both, but how they could be so polar opposites was beyond her. Michael gave her the least to worry about, but Maggie? This move might be harder on her more than she could have imagined. All she could do was to keep a close eye on her and show her as much attention as possible. With that, she finished off the cocktail, signed the check, personally thanked the server, then escorted Michael, his bag of books in hand, safely to the pool.

"I'll let your father know you're here. And if you need anything just ask one of the pool attendants. Okay?"

"Sure, Mom. I'll be fine."

The ladies left, Christine stopping first at the pool bar to inform the bartender that Michael would be spending a few hours poolside and to make sure he was all right.

Pulling away from the hotel, Christine asked Maggie: "Shopping or sightseeing?"

"Duh!" Maggie croaked.

"Shopping it is."

By four o'clock, they were back in the car, pulling away from the hotel, and heading home.

Michael sat in the back and stared at the pile of shopping bags taking up the space next to him. "Jeesh! You guys went wild!"

Christine smiled. "We didn't forget you." She glanced over at Maggie. "Give Michael his surprise."

Maggie searched through the additional bags that lay at her feet, finally finding the one. She handed it to him.

Michael ripped it open to discover a new iPad. "Oh! My! God!"

"Thought it would help you to do research on your subject *du jour*. And your sister helped me."

It wasn't often that her son remained speechless, so she enjoyed the moment.

"Thanks, Mom! Thanks, Maggie!" His excitement was palpable.

Christine saw Maggie break into a smile. Finally, everyone was content.

When they arrived home, Michael immediately ran to his room to play with his new electronics and Maggie to hers, to try on the new wardrobe. Christine went to the kitchen, then stopped cold. "What the…?"

Every drawer, every cabinet door was pulled out or opened. Obviously, this was not how she left the kitchen earlier.

Standing a moment to absorb the oddity of the event, she slowly began to move, pushing everything closed. Looking around, she realized nothing else was tampered with. *Maybe there's an odd angle to the house. An imperceptible slant that occasionally causes things to open*, she thought. Pushing it out of her head, she started dinner.

Stan arrived home just after seven, received his cocktail and took a place at the kitchen table. "Well, how was your day?"

"It was great!" she reported. "Spent some quality time with Maggie, spent a lot of money—but I told you I would—bought Michael an iPad. He deserves it," she said. "He's a good student and he'll get a lot of use from it."

"I agree," Stan replied. "A lot of money?" he added with a smile.

"Don't worry," Christine said with a laugh. "We'll still be able to pay the mortgage."

When dinner was ready, and the family had taken their chairs, Stan made the announcement. "That party we talked about? It'll be next week"

"Yes!" Michael screamed. "Hey, Dad, Mom got me an iPad. Thanks!"

Stan patted his son on the back. "Use it well, kiddo."

Maggie smiled. She was feeling more confident now that she had a new bathing suit.

"Dad," she said. "Did you leave your watch in my room?" She pulled his missing timepiece from her pocket. "I found it at the bottom of my closet when I was putting away my new clothes."

Stan, mystified, took the watch, and stared at it. "How did it get there?"

"Maybe it fell off your wrist when you were inspecting the closet the other night." Christine suggested.

"No. It was already missing from the night table. I wasn't wearing it."

"So," Stan said, purposely to refocus away from the watch. "You two will have to help your mom out with getting things ready for the party. Understood?"

In light of their newfound bounty, they couldn't refuse.

Christine made a bogus frown. "Always falls to the mom!" In reality, she loved organizing parties. It wasn't at all difficult for her. She had done so many in the past, both for her students as class events and for her own kids. It would be a cake walk.

"I'm also inviting Loretta. She might enjoy it."

After dinner, with dishes cleared, and the kids in their rooms, Christine considered telling Stan about the sight that met her in the kitchen on her return. But something told her not to, not now anyway. She refilled her wineglass and met him by the pool. It was still hot, but peaceful, and quiet. It was a good time to catch up with him.

"Thursday, I'll be all day in Palm Beach," he informed her. He took her hand in his. "Probably won't be home for dinner. You'll be all right?"

"Are you serious? With the party to organize, I won't have any time to not be all right. And I'm planning on stopping at the Garden Center, so I can start putting in trees. But I won't do that until after the party. I don't want the yard looking all dug up."

"Hey, do we still have that badminton net and rackets? We can set that up so people can play if they don't want to swim." His face took on an expression Christine read immediately.

"What's wrong?" she asked.

"Wrong? Nothing is wrong. Just weird."

"What do you mean by that?" she asked now intrigued.

"I asked my secretary to write all the invitations and to hand them out to the managers."

"Yes?" Christine asked, intrigued.

"A couple of them came to me to confirm our address."

"What's so odd about that?" she asked.

"They acted odd. Almost scared."

"Scared!?" She sipped wine. "Of what?"

"That's just it. I don't know."

"Oh, come on. Maybe they were just nervous that their new leader was inviting them to his home. Maybe they felt a little intimidated."

Frogs began their nightly chorus, and an owl, sounding far off, began its eerie hoot. Then from the direction of the swamp, they both heard a strange sound.

"What is that?" Christine asked.

Stan cocked his ear and listened. "It sounds like chanting of some kind."

"Yeah," Christine agreed. "It does. But who would be out there in the middle of the night chanting?" A little chill shot up her spine.

"Who knows?" he said. "Somebody's CD player?"

Christine remained at a loss. After another few minutes, it stopped as abruptly as it began. The frog chorus grew louder almost drowning the crickets that began as soon as the chanting had stopped.

"Nights out here in the middle of nowhere really aren't that quiet." She laughed and sipped more wine.

"Guess not. Let's lock up. It's late." As every night, together, they went from one room to the next making certain doors and windows had been secured. Since Maggie's fright, it had become a regular habit.

At the top of the stairs, Michael sat, iPad in hand.

"Why aren't you in bed?"

Michael stared down the steps with the strangest expression.

They reached him and sat down next to him. "What's the matter, buddy?" Stan asked.

"You won't believe me."

"Yes, we will."

Michael hesitated. "Okay. I was on the bed with the iPad when I felt someone watching me. I looked up and there was like, a shadow man."

Christine and Stan exchanged looks.

"What do you mean 'shadow man'?" she asked.

"He was a black shadow. I couldn't see the wall behind him. He just stood there, then moved away. Then he totally disappeared."

"Are you sure it wasn't a reflection from the windows. Did you have the TV on?"

"No, Mom. I told you I was on my iPad."

Stan listened quietly, allowing his wife to maneuver the situation. As a teacher, she had dealt with lots of kids and their personal experiences, good and bad. He considered her the expert.

"Did he threaten you?"

"No. I was just surprised."

"Are you all right now?" She squeezed his hand gently to reassure him.

Michael took in a deep breath and thought a moment. "Yeah, I'll be okay. I know it was nothing."

"Go back to bed. Leave a light on. And if you need us, we're right down the hall."

He gave each parent a hug goodnight and disappeared back into his room.

"I'll tell you," Stan said. "He's a trooper. When I was his age, I got the creepies if I saw a spider."

They left their bedroom door open—just in case—and together crawled under the sheets.

"What do you think he really saw?" Stan asked in a whisper.

"I haven't the vaguest, but I'm sure it's nothing that can't be explained." She rolled over, kissed him on the cheek taking in the remnants of his cologne, enjoying the fragrance. It calmed her to have him close to her.

"You have a long day tomorrow. Get some sleep."

CHAPTER 7

It was Sunday, the day of the picnic.

Christine arose early, eager to get the details in order. She dressed and went down to the kitchen to start arranging bowls for potato chips, dips, prepare the poolside bar, set up the badminton net that she found in the garage, anything and everything that would make the party fun.

When she entered the kitchen, she froze. Once again, every cabinet door, every drawer, was wide open. She stood, amazed at the scene, but also fearful of it. *Why is this happening?* she wondered.

It had to be her kids, playing a prank. Convinced now that they had been the perpetrators, she angrily stomped up the stairs and roused each of them. Maggie moaned at being awakened so early and dragged from the bed, latched to her angry mother's arm. She was led into her brother's room.

"Michael, wake up!"

Her son cowered against the pillows, never having seen her so upset.

"What did you two do last night?"

The kids exchanged glances.

"Come with me!" Christine marched them out of the room and down the stairs. "There," she said pointing at kitchen drawers and doors.

She saw her kids' expressions grow wide, their eyes like saucers.

"We didn't do this," they both said almost in unison.

Christine's breath came heavily. "Well, who did?"

Stan, awoken by the chaos, came up behind them. "Holy crap!"

"Did *you* do this?" she screamed at Stan.

"Come on, Christine. Don't be an idiot."

Her hands flew above her head. "Well, someone did it! Kitchen doors don't open by themselves. Especially twice."

"Twice?" Stan asked.

A big breath exited her lungs. "Last week. I didn't want to say anything. I just figured it had something to do with the house settling or an imperceptible slant in the floor."

Stan gestured to the kids, and they all began to close everything.

Christine, her hands on her hips, stood in the center of the kitchen, confused and a little frightened. So many things were happening: footsteps, men in closets, shadows on walls, missing watches. Now this! There had to be a rational reason. But there was no time to ponder all of it. They had a party to prepare.

The morning air was refreshingly cool and dry considering that they were in the midst of summer. She arranged plastic cups on the bar, stocked the shelf beneath the countertop with bottles of vodka, scotch, whiskey, rum, and gin. She slipped bottles of soda, assorted juices, and mixers in the refrigerator below. She decided she'd take the bag of ice cubes out of the freezer when people began to arrive.

By the time she finished, the kitchen was clear, and everything was back in its place. It was easier to maneuver the room now, prepping everything else. Hot dogs and burgers were in the fridge, bags of rolls and chips sat on top of the counter, waiting to be put in serving bowls.

She glanced out to the pool where Stan was arranging the extra folding chairs she had purchased at the Walmart. He looked so athletic in his white shorts; his blue eyes hidden behind the dark sunglass lenses. *He had only gotten better with age*, she mused. Then her mind refocused to the upcoming event. She hoped there would be enough seating. She realized she was both nervous about entertaining Stan's colleagues, some she had never met, yet excited at the prospects of throwing their first bash in their new home. Everything had to be as perfect as possible.

Finally, the first guests arrived. She and Stan met them at the door. Tanya was the housekeeping manager. With her was her husband Dallas, and their two small boys, Willy and Freddie.

"What a beautiful house," Tanya gushed upon entering the foyer.

"Boy," she said to Stan. "The hotel must be paying you a fortune."

"Actually," Christine replied, "we got more for our little house up in New York than what this place cost. Frankly, it was a steal."

They were escorted to the pool area and offered drinks.

Maggie sat, stuffed into her usual chair, earbuds attached to her head. Michael was testing the badminton rackets. He was eager to try his swing.

Within the next hour, most everybody invited had arrived. Many armed with housewarming gifts or bouquets of flowers.

Barbara and Allen Johnson stepped out into the sun. Their sixteen-year-old son, Ben, followed behind. He spotted Maggie immediately.

Maggie spotted him just as quickly. Suddenly, her demeanor changed. She touched her hair, adjusted her posture, sat up, refocused her attention away from her phone.

Uh-oh, Christine thought as she saw the two exchange glances, *I sense trouble.*

Ben migrated to where Maggie sat. He introduced himself, then sat on the edge of the pool, his feet dangling in the water. He invited her to join him. Maggie boldly left her chair and sat next to him. There was obviously some electricity flowing between them. Christine was happy to see Maggie enthused about something. On the other hand, it was a boy—one she learned was a bit older than her.

Stan manned the grill serving up hot dogs and burgers just as fast as they could be eaten.

A group of a dozen kids had wandered down toward the tree line, drawn by their curiosity of the swamp. These places always held mystery as well as secrets. A mysterious fascination.

Suddenly, one of them let loose a spine-chilling shriek. It set off a stampede of screaming children, racing back toward the house.

Adults jumped from their seats and quickly crowded onto the lawn to see what the commotion was all about. Stan, too, dropped the BBQ tongs and ran to see what was happening. Christine was in hot pursuit.

Michael pointed to something moving toward them from the undergrowth.

"Holy shit!" Stan said. Everyone came to a dead stop to gaze at the largest alligator anyone could ever imagine. It emerged from the swamp and was sidling at an impossible speed toward the house.

"Get back!" he ordered everyone. "Back to the house!" His arms flailed as he herded everyone back onto the patio.

The creature's ungainly body did not slow it down. It continued charging, closing in on the terrified guests.

"Dad, that thing is really aggressive. That's weird. Everything I've read about them says they are usually shy unless provoked or hungry."

"Did any of the kids throw rocks at it?" Stan asked, as he and Michael moved backward, closer to the house.

"No, Dad. It just appeared from the bushes."

The gator came to a stop about fifty feet from the patio. It stared at them, its huge jaw agape, hissing angrily.

Something caught Stan's attention as he continued to monitor the alligator. "Do you see that?" he whispered to Michael. His head nodded in the direction of the trees, a little to the right of where they were.

Michael squinted against the sunlight. "It's a man! What's he doing there? He's just staring at us."

Stan took Michael's hand, guiding him in a large circle around the animal and headed to the trees. But as soon as they got close to where the man should have been, they saw no one.

"That's freaky," Michael said. "Where did he go?"

Stan scanned the undergrowth. No one. They began to circle back again, noticing how the alligator remained fixed on their movements.

Several guests, by now, had corralled their children, made hasty thanks to Christine, and fled the house.

Christine didn't blame them. This could turn dangerous if anyone became careless.

Loretta arrived as guests were running back to their cars. *What now?* she thought.

Someone shouted, "Gator!" as they hurried to their vehicles.

Loretta entered the house and hurried to the yard to see what the commotion was about. She quickly sized up the scene, immediately grabbed her phone, scrolled and hit speed dial. Speaking quickly, she gave the address.

"Not the way I intended to entertain," Christine remarked dryly as she pointed to the beast.

Loretta's mouth fell open. "Holy crap! I've never seen one so big. What is it, eighteen, twenty feet? I already called animal control. Luckily they're just a few minutes from here."

"Thanks," Christine replied, keeping her eyes fixed on husband and son as they remained a safe distance from the animal. "Does it matter how big it is? What's a foot or two when you have a jaw like that?"

The gator began to move forward again, but slowly, less aggressively, toward the gawking few that remained.

Two men suddenly appeared from around the house, one unshaven, wearing a hat like the one worn by Dr. Jones in the *Raiders of the Lost Ark* movies; the other sported a baseball cap and was clean-shaven. Both wore denim shirts embroidered with "Gator Guys" on the right shoulder, overlaid with the logo of a smiling alligator.

Christine waved at them and explained how the thing burst from the undergrowth and charged across the lawn at lightning speed, frightening and endangering everyone.

"Wow," the unshaven man uttered. "He's a big one. But no worries. We'll snare 'em. We've been doing this for a long time. By the way, I'm Butchy. This here is Captain. Well, he's really not a captain, we just call him that."

Christine could only assume that he saw the frustration growing from her. She couldn't care less if they were named Marie and Donny Osmond, she wanted the alligator removed tout suit.

"Get everyone inside," Butchy said to Christine. "These guys can be unpredictable."

Christine called to Stan and Michael to get back to the house. The few remaining guests retreated inside to watch the action from the windows.

Butchy and Captain, a coil of rope and a spool of what looked like electrical tape in hand, carefully approached the gator. The gator opened its massive jaw revealing a set of sharp and menacing teeth. It hissed again as they neared.

Butchy made a lasso and began to attempt a capture. Three times, he failed to secure the rope either around the snout or the tail. The monster was becoming enraged. It made a false charge and then spun around and started back toward the undergrowth.

The two wranglers were now hurrying to catch up, made a few more failed attempts with the ropes, disappointed to see the creature disappear back into the safety of the swamp.

Stan tapped his son on the shoulder and indicated with a nod to the place they had seen the man. Michael could see them too. They wore things in their hair and some kind of plating over their chests. It was too far away to make out the details. A moment later, they were both gone. Michael glanced up at his father, his eyes wide with curiosity and fear.

Butchy and Captain, rewinding useless rope around their arms, approached Loretta and Christine who had reemerged from the house. The men were shaking their heads in disbelief.

"Ain't never seen that before," Butchy said to the ladies. "That thing just disappeared."

"You mean back into the swamp?" Loretta asked.

"No. I mean just disappeared. Like it was never there. No trail, no fading away into the swamp. Poof! It was just gone."

"Like it never existed," Captain added. "Never seen nothin' like it. And we've been doin' this for a good fifteen years."

After they gathered up everything they brought and finished the beers Christine had offered them, they disappeared around the corner of the house, back to their truck, vanishing as the gator had vanished.

"Just another mystery," Christine said to Loretta as they returned inside.

Maggie and Ben had watched the scene from her parents' upstairs bedroom window. So terrified of the huge reptile she couldn't even remain on the same level. She needed height between her and it. Then she saw the men again. She poked Ben in his side. "You see them?"

Ben stared hard to where her finger indicated. Maybe he couldn't find the right spot, maybe he was too slow. "I don't see anything but the gator running back to the swamp."

Christine appeared at the door. "This is where you two wandered off."

"Mom, that thing scared the heck out of me. Now we have those monsters to worry about?" She was about to ask if they could move back to New York, but something stopped her. The improbability? Ben? Maybe she found a new friend after all.

"Come on. Downstairs. Ben, your parents are getting ready to leave."

They followed Christine down the staircase into the foyer, where, indeed, Ben's parents were waiting.

Maggie hurried off, returning with a slip of paper. "Here's my phone number. Maybe we can go to the beach sometime."

Ben slipped it into his pocket. "Cool." He turned to Christine and Stan, who had been escorting the remaining guests to the door, and thanked them for a really great afternoon. "Can't wait to tell my friends about that gator!"

Maggie stood on the porch to watch Ben's family drive away.

Christine had seen Ben take the paper but wasn't overly concerned. Not yet anyway. "You know he's a tad older than you," she said when Maggie came out to the patio to help her mother and Loretta clean up. "I spoke to his mother. He'll be turning seventeen next month. You won't be fourteen for almost ten months."

Maggie shrugged but said nothing as she collected the paper plates and plastic cups littering the pool deck.

Then Christine looked over at Loretta. "By the way, why didn't your"—she lowered her voice to a whisper so Maggie couldn't hear—"lazy ass husband come?"

Loretta smiled. "He said he wasn't feeling very well, and besides, he said there was a *Bonanza* marathon on TV he wanted to catch."

She lied. He was keeping to his promise of never setting foot in the Minter's house, even if it was with a few dozen other people and in the middle of the day. That was all right with Loretta, but she couldn't tell Christine the truth or she would have to open that forbidden "can of worms."

Christine laughed. "Well, I hope Little Joe, Hoss, and the Ponderosa help make him feel better."

Once everything was cleared away and the kitchen back to a neat and orderly state, Christine poured Loretta more wine. If truth be known, she didn't want Loretta to leave right away. She enjoyed her company. She also decided that she should mention a few things, to get them off her chest and to get a second opinion.

It had gotten too hot outside, so they took seats on the antique couch in the rec room. "It looks old," Loretta said, brushing her hand across the brocade.

"It's old," Christine concurred. "About a hundred fifty years old and too old for this house. It looked great in the house in New York but out of place here."

"But it's comfortable," Loretta commented as she tested the cushions. "I'd buy it from you, but Lazy Ass would just move from his chair onto this and never move again."

The woman both smiled at the new nickname Loretta found for Matty. Then Christine's smile faded.

Christine took a sip of wine, then turned to face her. "I want to ask you something."

"Sounds serious," Loretta said.

Christine bolstered herself with yet another gulp and asked: "Do you know of any strange events occurring in this house?"

"Like what?" Loretta feared that 'can of worms' was getting ready to be opened.

"Well, the kids have been having some strange experiences. They claim they've been seeing things. Twice, I came into the kitchen and found every drawer and cabinet door wide open." She paused for a second. "A wristwatch of Stan's mysteriously disappeared, and then just as mysteriously, reappeared." She hoped she wasn't sounding as if she had a screw loose.

Loretta sat back, produced a deep sigh, and shifted her gaze to the wine glass, hesitating, wondering what she should say, the little she knew of the house. "Frankly, I've heard some people claim that stuff goes on here, but I don't know what they mean by 'stuff' and whatever it is, I don't buy into it. Every house has its own personality. You even told me that your house in New York made lots of noises."

"I suppose so," Christine whispered. "It must be my imagination."

She looked at Loretta who was still peering into the wine swirling in her glass. "Thanks. I needed that."

"And," Loretta added, impulsively, "no one died in here. That I can tell you without doubt."

Christine broke into a smile. "That is certainly good to know."

Stan appeared. "Are you two getting shnockered?"

Christine raised her glass to him, "I hope so!"

"I'll be in the garage. There're still a lot of unopened boxes to organize." Then addressing Loretta, "And thanks for calling those gator guys."

"My pleasure," Loretta replied.

"He is a god!" Loretta added after Stan was out of ear shot.

"You think so? Christine asked.

"Come on, girl! He is gorgeous with all that thick black hair, those blue eyes. And charming! He seems to be the best father the kids could ever have, and he doesn't treat you too shabby."

"You're right. How much luckier could I be?"

"Well, if you ever want to trade him for my Lazy Ass, you'll get no argument here."

Both women were laughing. The wine was doing its job. "And you're not going anywhere. There's another bottle we have to polish off."

"My ass is stuck to this hundred and fifty-year-old couch until the mission is accomplished."

Chapter 8

The next morning, Christine woke with a bit of a headache. *Too much wine*, she thought. Nevertheless, this was going to be the day she planned to visit the nursery. She couldn't let a little pain keep her from her agenda. But as she peered out the bedroom window at the sun-soaked sky, the temptation to just stay home and wait until the next day was too hypnotic. She threw back the blankets and crawled out of bed. Stan had already left for work and who knew where the kids were.

She slipped on some shorts, a light blouse, pushed her feet into a pair of sandals, and headed down the stairs to the kitchen.

A pot of coffee had already been brewed and still hot. *Such a good husband*, she thought. Pouring a cup, she then headed for the patio.

The morning was beautiful, the sun was bright, the humidity had lifted. It would be a perfect pool day.

Stan informed her at dinner the night before, that he would be running up to the Palm Beach hotel in the morning to see how it was doing.

"I'll be gone all day," he had told her. "I don't know when I'll get home with the traffic. But I'll call you later."

She wasn't surprised to see her son was already poolside, stuffed into a chaise, staring into his iPad. "Good morning!" she called from across the water.

Michael looked up briefly "Hi, Mom."

Maggie appeared at the door. "I'm going to beach with Ben."

Christine almost dropped the coffee cup. "Excuse me"

"Ben has a driver's license," she told her.

"I don't care what he has. You are not going anywhere with that boy." She felt her anger brewing. "I thought I made myself clear yesterday. He's too old for you!" It wasn't really her nature to get steamed up, so her reaction startled her.

"Why not?" Maggie asked, with an imperceptible stamp of her right foot.

"Because you are thirteen, he is sixteen."

"Going on seventeen," Maggie interjected.

"Can no one hear me!? You are too young. But more importantly, I said no." Christine turned back to gaze out toward the swamp. Her hand began to tremble. She placed the cup at her feet so as not to drop and shatter it. It was so unlike her, she knew. But the anger only grew.

"If we were in New York, you'd let me," Maggie said.

"No, I wouldn't," Christine countered. She took a deep breath and a moment to think. "If he wants to come over here, that will be fine. But you're not going to the beach unless your father or myself are with you. Or until you turn eighteen."

"I hate you!" Maggie snapped as she turned and ran back into the house.

Christine was shocked. Never had either child been so nasty. So defiant. Inside her head, she heard the word *bitch* but whether it was a reference to Maggie or herself, she wasn't certain.

Christine finally composed herself and continued staring at the trees. Yet the vision of that alligator popped back into head. *Would it return?* she wondered. Her eyes began to scan the end of the property, fearful that it might make another visit. In fact, she made a note to self never to let the kids out without some sort of supervision. Thankfully, Loretta had given her the phone number for the Gator Guys just in case the beast reappeared.

Her reverie was interrupted when Michael spoke up. "Mom, did you know that the Spanish were here hundreds of years ago? And that Cortes searched everywhere for the Fountain of Youth?" He looked over the screen. "Do you think there really was a Fountain of Youth?"

Christine shook her head. "No, sweetie. Back then people believed a lot of crazy things."

"Well, the Spanish were not very nice to the Indians who lived in Florida. They made them slaves, tortured them, killed them. Then they all started dying from the diseases they brought from Europe."

"That's another thing back then," she said, trying to remember her history. "The Spanish were more interested in finding gold and silver than being nice to the natives. Greed can be an ugly thing."

Michael fell silent as he continued reading.

Christine wished Maggie could be like him. Maybe he was a Mr. Know-It-All, but it was better than being a little bitch. There! There was that word again. She had never referred to her daughter or anyone else as a bitch. She shook off the thoughts and leaned her face into the sun, closing her eyes, hoping her wine-induced hang-over would lift.

She awoke to conversation from across the pool. Opening her eyes, she saw Maggie sitting on the edge of the pool, dangling her feet into the water, and beside her was Ben.

"Hello, Mrs. Minter," Ben called out when he saw that she was awake.

"Hello, Ben," Christine replied, relieved that Maggie had relented and chose the pool.

Ben wore a blue speedo, the muscles of his arms and legs were well defined, indicating that the boy must work out. His hair was the color of beach sand and pushed back away from his face to reveal, clear blue eyes and a smooth complexion.

Most kids that age were usually fighting the ever-dreaded acne, she thought. Then she felt something unexpected. She was getting turned on. *What!* she thought. *He's a boy!*

Suddenly she felt wicked, even corrupt. She forced her eyes back to the edge of the property, back to the scrub and palms. *I need to begin a mental plan of where the trees will be planted, where I'll put in flower beds. I need to get a book on indigenous plants that can be grown in this area.*

She shot up from the chair and headed back into the house, pausing only to ask if anyone wanted a drink. "Soda, iced tea?"

Ben waved, "Soda for me." Maggie and Michael asked for the same.

Christine entered the kitchen and froze. "Impossible!" she said aloud.

The refrigerator door was wide opened, everything was strewn onto the floor. Eggs were broken, fresh vegetables were thrown clear to the opposite side of the room. Milk dripped from the nearly empty shelves. "Kids!" she screamed.

The threesome ran into the house abruptly stopping when they saw what Christine saw.

"Holy crap!" Michael said. "What happened? Did you do this Mom?"

"Of course, I didn't," she replied, amazed that he would even ask such a question.

"Hey," Ben interrupted, his voice a whisper. "Could someone be in the house?"

Christine hadn't considered that, at least not until now. She automatically retrieved her phone from the kitchen table and dialed 911.

It took twenty minutes for the police to arrive. By then ice had melted into scattered puddles, ice cream into slushy blobs.

She met the lone policeman at the door and quickly led him to the scene. "We were out at the pool. All of us. I came in to get some drinks and found this." Her hand flew across her mouth as if to squelch a scream. "Maybe someone is in the house."

The officer took out a little notebook and jotted a few things and then ordered them to stay put. He unsnapped his holster and withdrew his weapon. He headed into the depths of the house as though he was familiar with the layout.

Christine, driven by her maternal instinct, herded the three kids close. Finally, what seemed to be an eternity, the officer returned to the kitchen.

"Nothing and no one," he said. "Everything is fine." Then he headed for the foyer pausing for a moment. "Just keep everything locked up."

He took a few steps and just before he exited, he turned and said, "You know, this isn't the first time I've been to this house for crazy things like that," referring to the mess in the kitchen. "Be safe." He was gone.

Maggie looked up at her mother. "What did he mean by that?"

"I don't know," Christine replied. "Come on. Help me clean things up."

Once all was back to order, they returned poolside. By now, dark storm clouds were swirling ominously above, blocking out the sunlight. Rumblings were shaking the eastern sky and a flash of lightning electrified the air.

"I think pool time is over," Christine announced, pointing up to the changing weather. Another snap of lightning flashed and crackled, chasing them inside. Rain came in torrents, sweeping across the lawn with such intensity that the yard was barely visible.

"Not like New York rain," Maggie bemoaned.

Michael stood at one of the windows in the rec room, staring curiously out at the tempest as if taking mental notes for the purpose of science research. He could hear the other three, still in the kitchen, where his mother was probably rescuing food from the refrigerator to turn into lunch. Then he felt something behind him. A presence. Then a sound. Breathing. He quickly turned, thinking that Maggie might be trying to scare him, but to his astonishment no one was there. He was alone in the room.

Shrugging it off to his imagination, he turned back to the window to find a face staring back at him. A pock-marked dark-skinned man, nearly naked, standing in the rain but amazingly not at all wet. An involuntary scream burst from his throat, but by the time Christine got to his side, the man was gone.

"He was watching me," Michael said, his finger elevated, indicating the spot where the stranger had been.

"Who was watching you?" Christine asked. Another snap of lightning shook the house.

"There was a man out there," Michael replied, his trembling slightly subdued. "But he wasn't getting wet." Adding, "He looked like an Indian."

"An Indian?" Christine repeated with disbelief. "Why would there be an Indian, standing out in the rain, *not* getting wet and staring at you. I think you've been reading too much about the Spanish and Florida history."

It seemed like a sensible excuse. "Yeah, maybe," Michael said. "He did look a little bit like some of the pictures of Indians I found on the website."

"Come on," Christine said. "Lunch is just about ready."

Stan arrived home late. Ben had left after the storm subsided and before it got dark, as were the conditions of his driver's license. The kids were already in bed. But Christine couldn't sleep. She sat waiting for Stan at the kitchen table, a glass of wine in front of her, mulling over the day. Things were getting weird. Unexplained kitchen messes, sounds, and now Indians. She heard the front door open and was relieved to see her husband enter the kitchen. He looked tired but wore a smile, indicating he was happy to be home. He kissed her hello and sat at the table with her.

"Drink?" she asked.

"Oh yeah," he replied without hesitation.

She debated whether she should tell him about the exploding refrigerator, but she hesitated. Yet sooner or later, he'd find out from one of the kids. So she bolstered herself to explain the strange event. But before she began, she stopped. Stan had placed a brown paper bag onto the table.

"What's that?" she asked.

He fell quiet, as if deciding whether he should show her or not. Then he spoke, "I know we discussed this, and I know your feelings but with the things happening and the isolation of this house, I thought it wise for all of our safety."

Christine set the glass of vodka and ice on the table and slid it toward him. "What is it, Stan?"

Slowly, he removed the object from the bag revealing a handgun.

"Oh no," was all Christine could utter. "Take it back."

"Listen, there was this place in Palm Beach. They show you how to use it. It would make me feel a lot better if it were in the house. Just in case. Worst case scenario."

Christine took a swig of wine and leaned back in the stool. She could see this meant a lot to him. After a moment, and against every objection she could think of, she relented. "All right. But the kids are not to know of it."

Stan nodded in agreement. "We'll keep it in our room. In the closet or drawer. Someplace where only you and I know its location." He slipped the weapon back in the bag, stood, drink in hand, and began for the staircase. "I'm beat. I'll see you in bed."

The room became quiet. Christine fell into thought. As much as she detested guns, maybe it wasn't such a bad idea to have a weapon in the house. If someone had gotten into the house earlier, she would have been better prepared to defend herself and the kids. And what if that alligator reappeared? At least, there would be a better chance of deterring it or even getting rid of the menace, that is, if the Gator Guys couldn't get to the house in time.

She refilled her glass and hit the weather app on her cell phone. It would be clear tomorrow. She could get to the nursery. She could get that gardening project started. She could get her mind off exploding refrigerators, knocks from the ceiling, and imaginary Indians. She could get on with her life.

CHAPTER 9

Michael arose early enough to see his father off to work and to join his mother for the trip to the nursery.

Christine left a note for Maggie on the kitchen table before they set off.

"It'll be fun," Christine said as they pulled out of the circle. "You can help me pick out the right plants that will grow well in this area."

Michael already had his iPad hard at work searching flora for South Florida.

A half hour later, they were pulling into the parking lot of Simpsons Nursery and Tree Farm.

"Wow! It's huge!"

Christine agreed as she peered at the size of the white metal-roofed open-air building with what seemed to be acres of flowering plants, trees, vines, and ornaments for the yard: glass balls, metal egrets, mini windmills—anything and everything.

A salesperson approached them, hands in dirty work gloves, blue jeans soiled at the knees, his forehead glistening with perspiration. He shot them a courteous smile. "Need some help?"

Christine smiled back. "We're new to the area, and I'd like to put in flowers and fruit trees. We have a lot of land."

The clerk smiled again and nodded.

"A friend of mine, Loretta, a real estate agent, recommended you. Said you would take good care of us."

"Loretta! Yes, everyone here knows her. She sends a lot of business our way. And yes, we will take very good care of you." After pulling the gloves off, he extended his right hand toward Christine. "I'm Lonnie."

"Christine" she replied, returning the handshake. "And this is my son, Michael."

"Okay," Lonnie said. "Might as well get started. Fruit trees, you mentioned?"

Christine nodded. "We're from up north, and I dreamed of picking an orange or grapefruit fresh from the branch."

Lonnie smiled at the notion as if it was the first time he had heard of such a dream. "Follow me."

He led them to an area behind the building. There were hundreds of assorted fruit trees, palms, so many trees she had never seen before.

He stopped at a clumping of pots and indicated that they were orange trees.

"They're not very big," Christine said.

"Once you get them in the ground, they should start producing fruit in a year."

"A year?" Christine asked.

"Sorry, ma'am. I guess you'll have to live off fruit from the grocery store until then."

"It's okay, Mom," Michael chirped in. "It'll be fun watching everything grow. You know it's not the destination; it's the journey."

Lonnie broke into a broad smile. "You got yourself a philosopher there."

"Yeah, he's my little scientist too."

They spent two hours under the hot sun wandering the building, choosing more trees, flowers, a shovel, a pair of work gloves, a sun hat, even an apron with pockets that she could wear over her clothes so as to minimalize the dirty factor. *Such beautiful trees*, she thought. Yellow cassia, lavender crepe myrtles, palms of all types. It was as tropical as it could get. When they had finally completed their mission and she was about to hand him her credit card, she hesitated.

"Can you deliver all this? There isn't enough room in my SUV."

"Of course," Lonnie replied, happy to add on a delivery fee. He spent a few moments making sure the order was complete and correct, then asked for the address.

"It's the house on Hawk's Bend."

Christine watched Lonnie's expression change, the smile disappeared, and his forehead wrinkled up. "Hawk's Bend?" he repeated.

"Yes," Christine replied. "Will that be a problem?"

Lonnie excused himself.

Christine and Michael exchanged quizzical expressions. Thankfully, a breeze arose to give a bit of relief from the humid stagnant air. Michael's straw-colored hair jostled in the wind and the sweat that had been beading along Christine's forehead evaporated.

A few minutes later, Lonnie reappeared with her credit card and receipt, handing them both to her.

"Will Thursday morning be all right?" No longer the smiling, friendly clerk he had been a few minutes before. He quickly thanked them and moved out of sight, to another side of the store, leaving a confused Christine to usher Michael back to the car.

*****

Maggie arose shortly after everyone left. Wrapped in pink terry robe, she stumbled down the stairs to get a glass of orange juice wondering where everyone had gone, that is, until she found the note left for her on the kitchen table.

Still sleepy-eyed, she opened the refrigerator door, found a carton of juice that had survived the earlier explosion, poured a glassful, then sat at the table to sip. Out of the corner of her eye, she saw something, a shadowy figure, dart past her and disappear into the rec room. Then a crash. She jumped up and cautiously made her way to the source of the sound discovering that a family photo had been knocked from a table and onto the floor, glass shattering everywhere. It was taken on a trip to Niagara Falls two summers earlier. Behind herself, parents, and Michael were the falls. The room had become as cold as a meat locker. She pulled the robe tightly around herself to quell the shivering that came not from only the cold but fear. Something was in the room with her. She could sense it yet saw nothing. Slowly, she stepped over the shards of glass and backed out of the room. It happened so fast. But something happened, she knew. Pictures don't go flying off tables by themselves.

Panic overwhelmed her. She raced into the foyer to the bottom of the stairs. The air around her seemed to liquefy. She struggled to move, but it was in slow motion.

"Help!" she screamed, knowing there was no one in the house to rescue her. Tears welled up in her eyes, and she grasped the railing to forcibly drag herself up. Every step took effort, until once at the top, the air turned light again, freeing her to run into her room, to her cell phone. As she sat at the edge of the bed, her trembling fingers punched the numbers to her mom's phone. Suddenly the room began to shake. Earthquake? Chairs slid across the floor, the bedside lamps slid off the tables and hit the floor. The closet doors swung open, and her clothes flew everywhere. But instinctively, Maggie knew this was no earthquake.

"Mom!" she screamed when she heard the phone connect. "Mom! Help me!"

Christine sped up and made it back to the house in fifteen minutes. Michael worried. Something wasn't right.

By the time they reached the circle, Maggie was on the steps, sobbing uncontrollably. Christine rushed to her, "What's wrong?"

Maggie, eyes swollen from crying, shook. She pointed to indicate something inside. Christine and Michael crept through the front door, noticing nothing. From what they could tell, everything was in place. Secretly, she wished she had that gun her husband had bought, but it was upstairs, on the top shelf of their closet.

"In my room," Maggie shouted from the porch.

They inched their way up the stairs, then to the left, to her daughter's room. The door was open. And when they stepped into the disaster zone that was Maggie's bedroom, they both gasped. The bed was no longer against the wall but in the middle of the room, books and papers blown to every corner. Clothing was ripped from the closet and drawers pulled open. It was surreal scene.

Could Maggie have done this? Christine wondered. Maybe acting out for not giving her the freedom she wanted. In her past teaching career, she had seen similar instances when children, stressed or revengeful, committed the craziest acts of hooliganism. What else could it be?

She returned to her daughter, sat down beside her and placed an arm around her shoulders "Are you okay?"

"No! No, I'm not okay. I just saw my room ripped apart like some invisible tornado swept through it, and I'm supposed to be okay?" Then she remembered the family photograph. "Look in the rec room. Something knocked the photo off the table while I was in the kitchen. Our vacation to Niagara Falls."

Christine thought for moment. That was her favorite family photo.

Maggie's demeanor changed. Her face radiated pure hate. In a voice Christine had never heard, she snarled, "Get out!"

Frightened, Christine jumped to her feet.

"What?" Christine asked.

The pupils of Maggie's eyes became opaque black. Another snarl left her twisted mouth "Get out!" This time louder and more threatening.

Michael stood in the doorframe, disbelieving what he was see-ing, hearing. This wasn't his sister.

In what seemed like seconds, her eyes cleared and returned to their natural green. "Mom," The voice was hers again. "I hate this house!"

"What just happened?" Christine asked.

Maggie had no idea what Christine was talking about and said so.

"You don't remember what just happened?" her mother gasped.

With a quizzical expression, Maggie shook her head. "Just that I hate this house."

Michael's mouth gaped in disbelief.

Christine immediately decided to stop the questions. If Maggie couldn't remember, then she'd drop it for now. "Come on. Get up and let's put your room back together."

"Mom! Did you hear what I said?"

Christine stood up, her shadow darkening her daughter's face. "Yes, I heard you. And whether you love or hate this house, this is where we're staying. So you'd better just get used to that." She turned and started for the door.

"Now get your butt up and help me with your room."

CHAPTER 10

The delivery from the nursery arrived first thing on Thursday morning as she had been told. The delivery man worked quickly unloading everything she had purchased, placing all the plants, tools, and bags of soil on the back patio, farther away from where she planned to plant everything. But when she tried to speak to him, he ignored her, hurriedly finished the job and headed back to the truck.

"Wait!" Christine called out. She waved a twenty-dollar tip at him, but he again ignored her, jumped behind the steering wheel, and drove off.

How odd, she thought. *Turning down money*. But she shrugged it off and returned to the back of the house to inspect her purchases. There was the shovel, the apron, which she picked up and tied around her waist, six twenty-four-inch pots, each containing a different tree: lime, lemon, orange, mango, avocado, and papaya. They averaged four to five feet in height, all appearing robust and healthy. The orange tree already had a few aromatic blossoms that promised that she might have some real homegrown fruit sooner than Lonnie had predicted.

It was time to go to work. First, she gazed out at the property. There was more land than she could have thought possible. In New York, their yard had ample space, but what she had now was more like a farm. She went inside to change into some shorts and a light work shirt. Finding an old pair of sneakers at the bottom of the closet, she slipped them on but before turning and walking away, she reached up to the top shelf, her fingers feeling blindly for the gun that had been hidden beneath some sweaters. The cold metal finally came into contact. She carefully withdrew it, aware that her husband had loaded it before storing it, which probably wasn't the best idea, but it was one step she didn't have to figure out. Cautiously, she placed it into the pocket of her apron rationalizing that she would be ready should that alligator reappear. She also grabbed her cell phone, checking that the number for the Gator Guys had been properly added to her contacts, then proceeded to head downstairs. Next, it was enlisting her son to carry the pots to the yet to be designated planting spots.

Thankfully, Michael was eager to assist and followed her out to the patio.

"Just get all the pots to the end of the yard, over there," she ordered, indicating the western edge of the property.

She walked ahead of him, shovel in hand, her attention interrupted by an occasional sound rising from the swamp. Fear of an alligator seemed to overtake her concerns of any events taking place inside the house.

The morning sky was cloudless and the sun hot. Beads of sweat began to appear along her upper lip and she wondered how long she'd be able to work under these conditions.

Surveying the area ahead of her, she quickly decided where her trees would go. She waved to Michael to bring her the first container. As he dragged the orange tree along the lawn, Christine took the first bit out of the earth. It was more compacted than she expected, her muscles strained to penetrate the land with the shovel. But at last, a hole existed, one deep enough.

Michael shook the roots free of the plastic pot and with Christine's help, positioned the plant upright.

Christine shoveled the dirt back around the tree trunk, tamping the loose soil with her foot, then stepped away to examine her work.

"Not bad," she stated proudly. It was the first tree she had ever planted. Okay, she had put in mums and impatiens in her New York garden, but never a tree.

Michael ran back to the patio to retrieve another pot while Christine paced off what should be about ten feet. The shovel bit again into the earth which seemed easier to manipulate. Each shovelful was placed in a pile next to the hole accumulating quickly as she dug. With another lunge, she heard a clink and felt something hard come in contact with the spade.

She put the shovel down and fell onto her knees. Digging with bare fingers, she excavated the bottom of the hole until she felt something metallic. Bringing it into the sunlight she brushed off the dirt and stared at it with shock.

"What's that?" Michael had come up behind her unnoticed, dragging the second tree, the mango.

"Not sure," she replied, seeing now how the sun gleamed from its surface.

Michael leaned in closer to look for himself.

"It looks like silver!"

Letters began to emerge from the filth.

"Look at this!" She handed it to her son.

"Mom, it's Spanish!"

"Can you read it?" Aware that he was not fluent, yet she asked all the same.

"Not this side of it, but on the other side are names." He flipped the thing over and read aloud "Francesca, Teresa, and Pedro." He noticed notches on the top. "I think it used to be attached to a chain."

A shiver-inducing wind came up suddenly and whipped around them. Wisps of clouds thickened above their heads.

"Where did that come from?" Christine asked, looking up at the sky. The weather was changing. Sounds began to emanate from the swamp. People speaking, but softly. They couldn't make out what was being said. The wind carried a growl that seemed to have come from deep inside the swamps. There was a kind of excitement or electricity in the air.

Michael trembled. "What's going on?"

Christine was on her feet again staring toward the source of all the sounds. The air had come alive. A cold breeze carried the cries of what could be animals. Her hand slipped into the pocket of her apron touching the muzzle of the gun. Then her fingers felt her cell phone. She wasn't certain which one would play a more important role should anything horrific occur. Then it became quiet. The cold air turned warm again. The amassing clouds seemed to dissipate. The sun returned to burn their bodies with its unforgiving heat.

"Let's plant this tree and go back to the house. We can finish the rest in the morning." She shoved her hand back into the apron pocket.

"Where is it?" She shrieked. "Where's that medallion?"

"Right here, Mom." He reached out his hand to her, the medallion in his palm. "It feels funny."

"Give me that!" Her voice was unusually angry.

"Okay, don't get mad."

She snatched it from his hand and gripped it with a fist. "Don't ever…ever touch it again."

Michael was surprised to see his mother suddenly become so agitated. And for what? Her cheeks had turned red, her eyes wild.

She did one last compacting pat with the flat side of the spade, securing the mango tree into the earth.

Without another sound, she dropped the spade, and headed for the house leaving her son behind.

Michael, confused and upset, watched her disappear into the house, then followed her inside.

Stan arrived home later than usual.

"About time," she snapped.

Stan flung his jacket onto the back of the chair. "I called you. I told you I was going to be late."

"Drink?" she asked, her voice calmer.

"Oh yeah."

She went to the refrigerator and filled a glass with ice and then poured vodka almost to the rim.

"How was your day?" Stan asked as he debated if he would be able to finish all the liquor she had served him.

"Finally got some planting done. A few trees."

"That's great!"

She took a long sip from her wineglass as she internally debated whether she should show him her find. At last, she reached into her pocket and withdrew the medallion setting it on the table between them.

"What's that?" Stan asked.

"Found it while I was digging."

He picked it up to inspect it more closely. "It's heavy. Feels funny."

"I know. Kind of weird."

"It looks like silver. Obviously Spanish. Probably pretty old."

"I found a place downtown that sells old coins. Maybe someone there can tell me a little more about it." She reached out and retrieved it from Stan. She became uncomfortable when it left her possession. Oddly, it seemed to have a hold of her, she realized. But that was ridiculous. How could some inanimate object sway such power? Nevertheless, it just felt better when she had it, in her pocket or in her hand.

"How was your day?" she asked. "Did you eat?"

"At the hotel. Good news. They found someone to manage the Palm Beach property, so except for a few trips up there to consult and get her settled, I won't have to make that drive any longer. You'll see a lot more of me. And I'll be home for dinner. We'll be a real family." He smiled but she did not smile back. "Are you okay with that? Thought you'd be happy."

"Of course, I'm happy with that."

"I'm exhausted." He managed to finish all the vodka she had poured, its euphoric effects dulling his brain. "Guess I'll hit the bed. Are you coming?"

"In a couple of minutes," she said, wrapping the fingers of her right hand around the stem of the wine glass. Her left hand unconsciously lay flat on the medallion, the skin of her palm feeling the tingling it weirdly emitted.

Stan grabbed the jacket of his suit that he had tossed onto the back of the stool, placed a kiss on her forehead, and disappeared from the kitchen. Yet as he climbed the staircase, he couldn't help but wonder about his wife's strange behavior: how she barked at him when he arrived home and her indifference to the news of his job. Maybe she was just tired, maybe it was the wine. Regardless, he was sure that after a good night's sleep she would recover.

As soon as he had left, something dark scooted past her and into the foyer. Christine, from the corner of her eye, got only a glimpse. It was black and amorphous, but it moved as if it had mass. Yet, it didn't instill any fear. She finished the wine in one swallow and followed in the direction it had gone. But she found nothing, heard nothing. So she turned out the kitchen lights and headed up to the bedroom, the medallion still tightly clutched in her hand.

CHAPTER 11

The next morning, Christine arranged to have lunch with Loretta. It had been a few weeks since they had shared a bottle of wine and Christine needed some adult conversation.

Before they were to meet at Café 5th Avenue in downtown Naples, Christine located the small stamp and coin shop she had researched a few blocks away. When she arrived, she read the sign that indicated that one must ring the doorbell for entry. She pushed the button, and a few seconds later, heard the click of the lock. She stepped inside. The shop smelled musty and the glass cases could use a dusting. She peered inside and saw the rare coins for sale. Many were quite old, as far back as ancient Greece. Many were Spanish. Along the walls were displays of stamps—thousands of them—protected in plastic. Stamps from every corner of the world. She could see why it was necessary to keep the door locked. Certainly, there was a fortune within these walls. But she wasn't there to advise the shop owner on housekeeping techniques or to purchase stamps or coins, she was there to see if he could give her some idea about the age, meaning and maybe value of the treasure she had found.

An older gentleman appeared from a backroom as soon as the door shut behind her. He smiled and introduced himself.

"Well, Mr. Weiler, I came across something while gardening and I was curious if you could give me some information about it." She reached into the pocket of her jeans and carefully withdrew it, noticing how it continued to emit that strange but subtle vibration. She said nothing about that fact and waited to see if Mr. Weiler would notice too.

The second she placed it into the palm of his hand, his expression changed. *He does feel it*, she thought.

"Interesting object," he stated as he brought it under a light and examined it more closely. It was a larger than silver dollar and about twice as thick. After a few moments of inspecting one side, he flipped it to inspect the opposite side.

"It kind of tingles," he said. "That's very odd."

"Yes, I noticed that too. I found it yesterday," She continued another moment watching him, trying to read his facial expressions. Finally, he set it back on the counter, if only to avoid the weird tingling effect.

"I've never really seen anything like this. Obviously, it's not a coin, though it is made from a very fine grade of silver. Those little notches give me reason to believe that a chain was once attached to it, maybe as a necklace."

"Can you date it?"

Mr. Weiler pursed his lips. "My guess, from the workmanship—which, by the way, is extremely good—to the engraving of the names and the words on the backside, it might go back to the sixteenth, maybe seventeenth century."

"Can you read that inscription?"

"Well, my Spanish isn't terrific, but I think it translates as 'My love will always be.'"

"That's rather beautiful," Christine said.

"You mentioned you found it while gardening. Do you live by the Gulf?"

"No," Christine replied. "We're about twenty minutes south of town, and about ten miles from the beach. Why do you ask?"

"Well, it's not often that old Spanish relics such as coins or medallions, like this, show up very far inland. Usually they're discovered in old shipwrecks, sometimes, out in the ocean, quite a distance from the shore."

Christine slipped the medallion back in her pocket and asked if she could pay him something for his trouble.

"No, nothing." He waved her off. "But should you decide to ever sell it, I can direct you to an auction house that specializes in old Spanish coins and such."

Christine shook her head. "I have no intention of selling it." She paused as she headed for the door, then hesitated. Turning back to Mr. Weiler, she asked, "If I were to sell it, how much do you think it's worth?"

Mr. Weiler thought a moment, attempting to consider its value which he had already done while looking at it. "Depending on the day, maybe, $50,000. If it had a provenance—you know, who owned it, who are Francesca, Teresa and Pedro, where it came from—it could be worth more. It's a unique item."

Christine caught her breath. *That's not chicken feed*, she thought. *That's a goodly sum of money*. Her breathing returned to normal quickly.

"I'll let you know." She smiled, left the shop, and walked the three blocks to the café.

Loretta was already seated at a window table, two empty wine glasses in front of her, an ice bucket by the side of the table chilling a bottle of chardonnay.

"I wasn't gonna start without you," she said as soon as she saw Christine walk in.

Loretta stood and the two exchanged hugs. "How are you?" she asked, noticing the pallor of Christine's skin. "Are you okay?"

"Yes, yes," Christine replied. "I just had a surprise, a good one, and I'm still digesting it."

The waiter hurried over to open the wine, pouring both equal shares, mentioning the daily specials as he did so, then scurrying away to give them a chance to make their decisions.

They clinked glasses, then sipped. Cold and refreshing.

"I have something to show you," Christine said, reaching into her pocket, removing the medallion, anxious to let Loretta in on what had happened. Placing it on the table between them, Loretta leaned in for a closer look.

"Where did that come from?"

Christine told how she had found it while planting a mango tree, and how the air became windy and chilly just as she pulled it from the earth. How she had just taken it to be examined by Mr. Weiler and what he said it might be worth.

"And," she added as if there couldn't be any more. "Hold it," she said hesitantly.

Loretta looked at her quizzically not quite comprehending.

"Pick it up."

Loretta complied, taking it up with fingers and placing it in the palm of her hand where she could examine it more closely. "Wow, it's a beauty." Then her expression changed. "Is that me or is this thing tingling my skin? Like it's alive!"

Christine leaned back. "It happened to Mr. Weiler too. Strange, huh?"

Loretta dropped it back onto the tabletop. "Strange? I don't think I like it. Medallions aren't supposed to do stuff like that. Put it away."

Christine shrugged and slipped it back into her pocket.

Loretta took another sip of wine and stared at Christine. "Fifty thousand dollars? That's a small fortune."

"You're telling me. But I'm not planning on giving it up. Maybe I'll just keep it so it can be a nest egg for the kids."

The waiter returned. "Have you decided?"

"No!" Christine snapped.

The waiter hurried away.

"You don't have to be nasty, Christine."

"Nasty?" Christine asked. "What do you mean?"

"You practically bit the waiter's head off with that tone." Loretta regarded her friend closely and wondered what was happening. This wasn't the Christine she knew.

Several minutes later, the waiter returned once more, approaching the table slowly, tentatively, uncertain what reception he would get.

Loretta looked up and smiled at him. "Yes, we're ready."

At last, their salads arrived, and conversation turned to the kids. "Maggie is becoming difficult, especially since meeting Ben. I don't know if she's acting out, but when I got back from the nursery her room had become a disaster. She said it was as if an invisible tornado ripped through. Yet I can't imagine her doing such a thing."

Loretta wasn't sure how to respond. Instead, she quietly contemplated the pieces of grilled chicken in the salad and sipped more wine. "Just be careful," was the only thing she could say.

Christine wanted to ask why but changed her mind. If Loretta had a reason, maybe she didn't want to hear it. Afterward, they chatted about Loretta's sales. Real estate was not doing well that year, although she had a lot of irons in the fire. She mentioned her husband, Matty, and how he was still doing nothing in his job search. Things at home were become a little tense.

"But sooner or later everything will work out," Loretta believed. "Things always do."

"Thanks for meeting me," Christine said when the check had been paid and the bottles of wine emptied. "I really love our friendship."

Loretta gave her a hug. "As do I. Hey, let's do this once a week."

Christine returned the hug and agreed.

With that, they left the restaurant and parted ways, Christine to her car, Loretta to hers.

Once back at Hawk's Bend, Christine considered continuing the planting of trees, but thought otherwise. The weather had turned iffy and the wine was making her lazy.

Michael greeted her at the door. "Did you have a good time?"

"It was very nice. Where's Maggie?"

Michael hesitated until his mother prodded him further for a reply.

"I don't know," he said. "She said she was going to the mall."

"With whom?" But Christine knew exactly with whom. Ben!

She took out her cell phone and called Maggie's number. No one answered.

Michael crept away. His mother's newfound temper was fomenting, and he didn't want to take the brunt of it. He grabbed his iPad and hurried out to the pool, hoping any storm brewing would come later than sooner.

Christine went to the refrigerator and took out a bottle of wine. Not that she really needed more, but something had to keep her calm.

After an hour, a car pulled up to the front of the house. Christine, feet spread, hands on hips, was there to greet her daughter's return. As soon as she climbed the front stairs, Christine ordered her to her room. Surprisingly, Maggie did not argue but obediently climbed the stairs to her room. Meanwhile, Christine approached the vehicle, to the driver's side, where Ben nervously sat, uncertain what was going to happen.

"Ben," Christine began as calmly as possible. "It's obvious you and my daughter like each other but it's also obvious that you're a bit too old for her."

"Just by a few years, Mrs. Minter," he said softly, smelling the wine on her breath. He kept his eyes focused on the steering wheel.

"It may be a few years, but those few years are a huge gap in maturity." She paused, then said, "I don't want you seeing Maggie, that is, unless a parent is with you. Hers or yours. Doesn't matter. Do you understand?"

Unexpectedly, a flush came over her. She had experienced it before, by the pool. The way his blondish hair fell over his forehead, the biceps stretching the short sleeves of his shirt. And his eyes, a clear blue that pulled her in. She turned her head for a moment, glimpsed at the bubbling fountain. This was ridiculous. Unnatural. Even evil. Pulling herself away from the car, she quickly hurried back to the front door, purposely not turning to watch him drive away. Now she had to deal with her daughter.

Maggie sat on her bed, knees pulled up to her chest. The television was on, but the volume turned off. Some paranormal program was on, ghost hunters seeking spirits in an old mansion. But she watched blankly, incapable of concentrating even on the mute visions of people and cameras searching musty rooms and hallways. She could only think of what the consequences of her disobedience would be.

Finally, the door flung open. Christine stood rigidly in the frame, appearing taller than her five-foot three-inch height.

"Really?" she said. The seed of anger, already germinating. "Why?"

"I had to get out of here! I hate this house." Maggie's eyes stayed glued to the television.

"You've already made everyone very aware of that. But you disobeyed me." Christine picked up the remote and turned the set off.

"Look at me!"

Reluctantly, Maggie turned her frightened gaze toward her mother.

"I want the truth. Has anything gone on, physically, between the two of you?"

Now Maggie was staring directly into Christine's eyes. "*No!* Nothing. We're just friends. I wouldn't do that. I'm not stupid."

"I told Ben and I'm telling you. If the two of you want to 'hang out,' there had better be one of us or one of his parents in tow. Understood?"

Maggie's expression changed to panic. "You told him that?"

"Yes."

"I am so embarrassed." She hid her face in her hands and then lifted it. The jaws muscles became taught. "I hate you!" she spat.

"I don't care." Christine went to turn away, finished with what she had to say, when she heard a growl. She turned back to see Maggie on her hands and knees, her face contorted, her eyes black, staring at her with what she could only describe as consummate evil. It was like the time on the front porch.

"Get out!" she growled. "Get out or die!"

It wasn't Maggie, Christine realized. The transformation was shocking.

Christine backed away, into the hallway. Her daughter had turned into a wild animal, ready to attack. Then it was over. Maggie relaxed and lay back onto the pillows.

"What was that?" Christine asked.

"What?" Maggie asked in her own voice.

Christine could see that she had no inkling as to what had just happened.

Christine could say nothing more. She closed the bedroom door behind her and returned to the kitchen where she poured more wine. Sitting, the soothing wine subduing the trembling, she pulled out the medallion from her pocket.

What was going on? she wondered. Maybe there was something wrong with the house. Maybe they should get out. Her fingers squeezed around the medallion. Like the wine, it too calmed her.

◯

CHAPTER 12

November 1640

The hand of Juan Hector de la Sola gripped the medallion that hung from his neck. It was the one thing in the world that gave him solace. His fingers wrapped lovingly around the precious silver, pressing his fingertips to the names of his wife and children—his family—many miles away, back in Spain. He had done it so often he could tell which name his finger was pressing against without glancing.

The morning was bright and cloudless, the sea calm. A balmy breeze fluttered the sails as his ship, *La Valencia*, set on a northwesterly course. Her bow cut cleanly through the waves. Dolphins cavorted in and out of her wake, breaching the white foamy waters like acrobats.

He was fortunate to receive this commission. His last, he swore. After he had completed this delivery of goods to the settlement at Tampa Bay, he would finally return home, to the warm embrace of Francesca and the smiles of his children, Pedro and Teresa. He hadn't been home in over a year. He could only imagine how grown the children must be.

La Valencia was a good ship. An eighty-ton carrack, not unlike the *Santa Clara*, known by her nickname *La Nina*, the ship used by Columbus, less than one hundred fifty years earlier. Over those years, much of the southeastern coasts of this new world had been visited. But unlike Christopher Columbus who never set foot on this new world, reaching only as far as the Bahama Islands, others had better success, making it to this land called La Florida, named for the Pascua Florida or the Easter feast of flowers.

After much of the eastern coast was surveyed, settlements began springing up along the western coast. Tampa Bay and Pensacola became necessary to protect Spanish holdings from falling into the hands of the invasive British, French, as well as marauding indigenous peoples.

A little more than a year had passed since any news had come from the Tampa Bay settlement. The governor had petitioned that a supply ship be sent, to bolster the soldiers who were there and to acquire what news of them. Juan Hector, recommended as a solid, able, and capable ship captain had been summoned to La Fortaleza, the governor's San Juan home. Juan Hector approached the impressive building, now fully recovered from the fire set by retreating Dutch fifteen years before. He paused for a moment to admire the grand fortress then headed to the entry way.

An aide led him to a small office where he was seated and told that the governor would join him shortly. Several minutes passed when the door swung open to reveal a short gentleman, his face partly concealed by a large but neatly trimmed moustache. Captain General Inigo de la Mota Samiento nodded a welcome and then seated himself across from Juan Hector. Juan Hector felt some nervous moisture trickling from behind his left ear.

"I think you know why I beckoned you here."

Juan Hector nodded as his hand moved unconsciously to his chest, gently touching the medallion that was hidden beneath his cotton shirt. "Supplies to the Tampa Bay colony."

The governor nodded and slid open a drawer. He withdrew some papers and slid them across the smooth mahogany desktop.

"These will be the official papers of passage which I have certified. Keep them with you always." Then turning the subject away from the voyage, he commented, "You hold tightly to whatever hangs from your neck."

Juan Hector paused, unaware that his habit of embracing his most valued possession had become obvious.

"Yes, *señor*," he quietly replied as he withdrew it from inside his shirt. "It has much emotional and spiritual value to me, more than what the silver itself is worth."

The governor smiled with a comment of how beautiful it was then slid a few more sheets of paper toward Juan Hector indicating that he would need a signature.

Juan Hector returned the medallion to his chest, picked up the pen, and with only a brief perusal of what was the usual format, he scrawled his signature at the bottom of the contracts, entrusting him as the captain of *La Valencia*. A feeling of satisfaction swept over him. It had been a few years since he had his own ship, running cargo from the seaports of Spain to numerous other ports along the Mediterranean seacoast.

It was less than a week later when he took command of his ship. Crewed with twenty-nine handpicked men and the holds brimming with supplies needed at the settlement, *La Valencia* set sail to the northwest, toward La Florida. It would be a voyage that should take no more than three weeks, if the winds were good and the seas tranquil.

It took days to assemble the supplies and load the ship: salted meat, hardtack, dried legumes, salt, sacks of yucca flour, lemons and limes, barrels of wine (to placate his crew and uphold their morale), tools, too: saws, hammers, adzes. Cordage and rope and large bundles of wool blankets, as well as bolts of cloth. The live animals proved to be a challenge. At first, the din of the chickens and constant squealing of the pigs was, in time, replaced by the stench rising from their pens below. Due to such reek, and the clement weather, the crew took to sleeping outdoors on deck, some in hammocks, to escape the choking vapors below.

Their voyage took a familiar route bypassing Hispaniola, then through the channel with Great Inagua, one of the Bahamian islands, to the north, the coastline of Cuba to the south.

Eventually, one uneventful day after another, Juan Hector rose early to scan the horizon. He placed the telescope to his eye to find that directly ahead, land masses were rising on the horizon. *Los Martires—The Martyrs*, Juan Hector thought.

A hundred years before, Ponce de Leon had named them such since they appeared to him to resemble suffering men. Juan Hector didn't quite see what de Leon thought he saw, but he knew that to get around to the western coastline of Florida, he would have to navigate between the islands. He squeezed his medallion and thought of his family. Every day, every week, that passed, was time closer to them. He would be back in Sevilla, money in his pockets and his life, once again with his beautiful family.

He made the decision to take the route between the Marquesas and the Dry Tortugas, through the Grand Boca Channel. That way he would be assured of deep water, and away from any of the islands that were said to be inhabited by Indians, who may or may not be friendly. Then he would swing north and travel along the west coast until he arrived at Tampa Bay.

All seemed to be well, the crew admiring the island chain but keeping aware of any problems that could occur and hinder their speedy passage. Without calamity, they made it through, then turned northward to follow the western coast until they made destination.

But as they drew closer to land, the seas began to become rough, and a westerly wind had sprung up.

Carlos de Vacas, a well-read, educated crew member who was often used by his captains as a translator, positioned himself next to Captain de Sola. De Vacas had spent some years among the Tequesta Indians on the eastern coast and had become proficient in their language and customs. He also became expert at reading the weather patterns of this tropical part of the world.

"This is not a good sign," he stated, looking out to the building sea.

The captain could only nod. After so many weeks of perfect weather, why would God do this now? Besides, it was near the end of November. The time of year when tropical storms and hurricanes were known to subside.

But they were fast approaching the barrier islands of Charlotte Harbour, the white caps rising higher. Perhaps they could make a safe landfall before the storm became too destructive.

Orders were given, and as the crew began to scurry about, lashing down everything and anything that could be blown overboard, the skies grew darker with banks of menacing clouds. The rain began to pelt the ship, at first vertically, then as the storm grew more treacherous, horizontally.

Claps of thunder, so deafening, that it drowned out the frightened squealing of the pigs.

Hours passed, and the winds blew harder. *La Valencia* listed to one side and then the other. So far, she was handling well and gave no signs of distress. The hours elapsed.

Then with what seemed to be a blessing from heaven, a hole of blue sky appeared. It was the eye, but it would be of no blessing what was going to happen next.

"Great trouble," Carlos said to Juan Hector once the silence fell upon them. "The worst of it is about to begin. I have been in these hurricanes before."

Juan Carlos directed the pilot to bring the ship as close to shore as possible and with all possible speed, or as fast as the storm would allow them, follow north along the coast, putting in at the first island that came into view, if one could be seen through the approaching darkness of night and the blinding sheets of rain. But it was of no use. The fiercest side of the hurricane came upon them and like a child's toy boat, swept *La Valencia* toward land. The tiller cracked. The ship was no longer maneuverable. They were at the mercy of the storm and God.

Suddenly, a great shudder vibrated through the ship. The sharp cracking of timbers induced terrified shrieks from the men. Unseen in the darkness, *La Valencia* had run aground. The hull shattered against the rocky shoreline. *La Valencia* listed to the starboard. Masts snapped, barrels and crates on and below deck shifted, sliding into the angle of the list, forcing all weight to one side. Juan Hector could feel the sudden drag as the keel, or what was left of it, slid across the invisible beach.

He had no other choice but to order all to abandon ship. Men grabbed what little they could. And the chaos began. The night darkness was fully upon them. Terrified, soaked, and rain-blinded, they began leaping overboard, screaming to God to have mercy on their souls.

The foremast snapped and landed on deck, missing a few sailors who were escaping. The loose wood rolled into the sea. Shredded sailcloth hung fluttering for a moment above the deck, then like phantoms, blew out to sea.

Pigs and chickens, freed from their smashed pens, either drowned or managed to make it onto the beach.

Juan Hector grabbed his medallion promising that this would not keep him from his family. Somehow, someway, he would get through this ordeal and make it home. Little did he know what awaited him.

Finally, with every man off ship, safe on shore, or drowned by the raging sea, Juan Hector gripped the railing and peered down at the angry surf shifting the golden sands below. The wind continued to blow in great gusts. It wasn't the leap that caused him hesitation since it was a mere six feet to the surface of the water, it was the fear that this moment was going to have a great and devastating effect on his life. What will now become of him and his men, of the plans he had of reaching home and family? Regardless of the promise he made to himself, that he would indeed return home, the reality of what lay before him was daunting. Lost in an unfamiliar land without any rescue. Fear was beginning to grip him, but he fought it off. He was not the kind of man who gave into impossibilities quickly. Without another thought, he leapt into the swirling waters, into the unknown, his feet sinking into the soft sand. Slogging his way onto dry land, he joined the surviving crew mates huddling as best as they could, their backs to the wind and the rain, sheltered by the rocks that had brought their ruin, watching *La Valencia*, ripped apart, one timber at a time by the ferocious winds and unforgiving sea.

Night turned into day, and after what seemed like forever, the wind slackened, the rain became nothing more than a drizzle, and soon, the clouds cleared to reveal a blue crystalline sky. The sun, now a blinding yellow ball, blazed down on their soaked bodies. The storm was over, as was their venture.

Juan Hector saw that the men were stunned by the event, some sat in the sand, motionless, mute, blank stares, reacting to nothing. Some wept. Others wandered the beach, despondently picking through the remains of *La Valencia* that hadn't been washed away. Some took it upon themselves to chase after the few animals that survived. Chickens scattered across the beach. The pigs, reveling in their newfound freedom, retreated into the dense mangrove forest that stretched along the strand.

Juan Hector counted. Out of twenty-nine men, only ten survived. He suggested that they gather rocks and build a memorial to those who did not make it.

One sailor pointed down the beach. Several bodies had already washed ashore.

"They need to be buried," Juan Hector said. "Their poor souls are in God's hands now."

Two who had been searching for the remains of *La Valencia* took on the job. They dragged the bloated corpses onto shore to a safe place far up from the water line. The day was turning hot, and flies were beginning to congregate on the dead sailors. There wasn't much time.

"We'll wait a little longer to see if others wash in. Then we will honor them all."

"Sharks probably got the rest," one sailor speculated.

It was a truth Juan Hector could not deny. These waters, it was said, were teeming with the monsters. Many sailors, tossed into the sea, became sustenance for such creatures.

Juan Hector turned somberly to face the survivors and told them that he blamed himself for such a disaster. But to the man, they disagreed.

"You did not create the storm," one said. The others nodded.

"Only God could do such a thing."

"Maybe we have made God and the Blessed Virgin unhappy," another suggested.

After that, everyone fell silent. Only the waves, now peacefully lapping at the sand, porcine squealing that grew more distant, and the bird calls emanating from the forest broke the stillness.

Later that day, after only one more body washed ashore, did they manage to find a patch of clear land away from the sand where they gathered together their departed comrades. They could find no tool to dig the soft, loamy dirt so they laid the dead together side by side and began to bury them by piling rocks and boulders on top to form a cairn.

Someone found a piece of wood, once part of *La Valencia*, and with his knife blade, etched in the names of those deceased. More wood was found to be fashioned into a cross.

Juan Hector stepped forward, his head lowered, his short beard and curly black hair speckled with beach sand and began: "We offer up these brave souls to you, O Lord, so that they may spend eternity safe within your loving arms." He faltered and stepped away. This was not how this voyage was supposed to go, and despite what the survivors said, he still felt the guilt for their deaths.

The focus now was to find food and water. Fortunately, enough was salvaged from the ship to give sustenance for a while. Chickens had been corralled and would be a good source of meat and eggs. A fire had been started, and a barrel of wine had been rescued. Miraculously, as if God was protecting them, a fresh water source, a small stream, was located only a few yards from the beach. As bad as things were, they could still maintain hope.

On the morning of the fourth day, they appeared. Three of them. Though they stood among the palms and scrub, they did not try to hide themselves.

Juan Hector's men stared back, uncertain of the strangers' motives.

As captain, Juan Hector was obliged to approach them. He asked Carlos to accompany him, since he may have the ability to communicate with them. Together, they slowly moved along the strand, never once taking their eyes from their unexpected guests.

Juan Hector had never seen Indians such as these. Their hair was black and long, some piling it upon the tops of their heads like beehives, others let it flow down their backs. All were festooned with strings of seashells of all manner. Round disc-shaped plates hung from their necks, covering their chests like armor. Their faces had been decorated with dabs of ocher and black. Each carried a spear, long and slender, attached to a frighteningly sharp blade.

"Do you recognize these people?" Juan Hector asked Carlos.

Carlos shook his head. "No. But my guess is that they are the Calusa."

Juan Hector nodded. "The 'fierce people'? I have heard of them." A chill passed through him. This could be more trouble. He recalled the writings of Juan Ponce de Leon whose men once skirmished with people of this tribe. "We must be cautious."

As they drew near, Juan Hector stretched out his hand in an offer of friendship and to show them that they carried no weapons.

The gesture was met with a blank stare.

Then one of them pointed a finger away from the beach and said something Juan Hector could not understand. But Carlos, from his years with the Tequesta, managed a few words.

"They said that we are to go with them," Carlos translated.

"Where?" Juan Hector asked.

Carlos waited until the man spoke again.

"To their camp."

Juan Hector felt his fear. "Do we have a choice?"

"I don't think so," Carlos replied as he nodded a consent.

Juan Hector returned to his crew. He called out for Diego and Cesar and ordered them to join Carlos and himself. The others, he said were to stay behind to salvage whatever they could and to keep a keen eye on the sea should any other ships happened to pass by.

Reluctantly, the six remaining crew men, stepped back as the two who were called stepped forward to follow their captain into an uncertain future.

A gesture indicated that the Spanish men should follow them. The remaining crew watched as the motley group disappeared into the trees.

All morning, they trekked through forest of palmetto, bald cypress, and gumbo limbo. Juan Hector had never been so deep into the Florida forest before. Orchids and air plants clung onto trees as did the huge variety of bromeliads. He, of course, did not know the names of these plants, but he was amazed at their beauty and the variety of their shapes and color. And he now understood how this land received its name: the abundance of flowers.

Sometimes, Carlos would remember what a flower was called in the Tequesta language. He pointed to a swath of muhly grass.

"The Tequesta use that for weaving baskets," Carlos said.

Other than the short botanical lessons, the Spaniards followed quietly, not knowing what their fate might be.

Juan Carlos assumed that if the Calusa wanted to murder them, the deed would have already been done. It was a comforting thought, one that would make his journey easier.

By midday, they reached a river where several canoes waited.

Juan Hector and his men were directed with hand gestures to climb inside. When they had been separated into two of the three boats, the Indians climbed aboard, dropped their spears for long poles. They then thrusted the ends into the shallow streambed, pushed away from shore. Propelling along the stream that grew wider and deeper, Juan Carlos couldn't help but marvel at the variety of wildlife.

Dazzling white-plumed egrets, incalculable in numbers, colonized the trees along the banks, blue herons, with wingspans of five feet soared overhead. A wild boar, appearing for only a moment, dashed from view as the boat made its approach. Juan Carlos knew now what the plight of his lost pigs would be—they would become feral and live out their days in this place.

Carlos, who sat behind Juan Hector, tapped the captain's shoulder, and pointed across the water.

Juan Hector turned his attention to the strangest and most frightening creature he had ever seen. It resembled a huge lizard, at least twenty-five feet in length, with a jaw of sharp dagger like teeth. Juan Hector's pulse quickened.

"What is that?" he whispered.

"The Tequesta call it an alligator. They are revered and very dangerous. It is a symbol of strength and cleverness."

"It could swallow a man whole!" Juan Hector whispered.

As the voyage continued into the afternoon, they saw many more of these creatures until they became commonplace. Juan Carlos would not want to be lost and alone out among these devils. His hand clutched his medallion.

At last, they arrived at what seemed to be a small makeshift dock. The canoes were met with dozens of other tribal members, all festooned with shells, their faces decorated with varying designs and colors. Women, their naked breasts barely covered by shell necklaces, their hair adorned with flowers of the forest and strings of colorful beads. These people were dark-skinned, causing Juan Hector to see how pale the Spaniards were in comparison. So far, the Calusa demonstrated no aggression toward them, maybe, if anything, a little curiosity. He had no idea if this group had ever been in contact with Europeans before. Nevertheless, all seemed to be going well.

They were led to a hut, low and circular, constructed out of palm fronds. They were ushered inside and motioned to sit on the woven mats that covered the packed earthen floor. Before long, another Indian joined them. Juan Hector saw the respectful head bows the others gave him as he entered and sat across from the Spaniards. It was clear by the others' reverence he held a position of importance, probably the chief. He stepped onto a small dais, built to be above anyone else and sat.

After a few moments of inspecting these strange white foreigners, he began to speak.

Carlos listened intently, attempting to understand all that he could. The language of the Calusa had many similarities to that of the Tequesta, but certain words remained untranslatable.

Unconsciously, Juan Hector's hand located the medallion again, hidden by his shirt, now filthy and moist with perspiration, and grasped it. The coolness of the silver and the knowledge that it was his closest contact with his family calmed him.

"He is not only the chief of these people," Carlos whispered. "He's made it clear that he is the chief of all Calusa and a powerful figure among his people."

Juan Hector let go of the medallion and placed his hand back on the lap, created by his cross-legged position.

Then to Juan Hector's dismay, the chief took a sudden interest in what he had been touching, the thing now shrouded by his shirt.

"He wants to see your medallion," Carlos said cautiously, aware of its importance to his captain.

Juan Hector hesitated, then slowly revealed it, pulling it out from under his shirt.

The chief leaned forward and peered at it for a moment, then leaned back, seemingly uninterested in such a thing.

A small almost inaudible breath of relief issued from Juan Hector's lungs.

The chief resumed speaking and after some time, paused to allow Carlos to interpret.

"He wishes us welcome. A hut and a meal will be prepared for us."

They were asked the purpose of their presence in Calusa lands.

Carlos, with carefully chosen words, explained that they were on a mission to restock the Tampa Bay settlement. They were ordered by *their* chief to do so. "And we come unarmed."

The chief seemed to react to the name of their destination. Maybe his people had fought other Europeans there. He then abruptly stood and with the other Indians, vacated the hut, leaving the Spaniards alone for the first time all day.

"Should we be concerned?" Cesar asked. Juan Hector chose Cesar for his bravery, preparedness, and the ability to stay cool under any circumstance. With the Indians gone, he tapped the leather bag he had strapped around his shoulder. "I brought a pistol."

"I only hope you don't need to use it," Juan Hector said.

By evening, the firepit in the center of the settlement had been set ablaze. The women were already preparing the meal: fish, shellfish, squash, corn, and other foodstuffs the Spaniards could not identify. It didn't matter. None had eaten the whole day and their stomachs were crying out to be filled.

Some women sat close to the firepit, tossing fish and vegetables into a large cauldron resting upon the burning embers of the fire. Aromas began to rise into the air and the Spaniard's mouths watered.

As they waited, Juan Hector, peered at the village around them. There were dozens of huts, much like the one where they had met the chief. From his calculations, the encampment population must be between one hundred and two hundred people.

It seemed their arrival created either a reason for celebration or simply over-the-top hospitality. The captain was quite pleased that their appearance was being well accepted. But he also knew that they could not stay with the tribe forever. They would have to make plans to seek out direction and the fastest way to the closest Spanish settlement. The captain's thoughts turned to the men he left behind. If he were rescued, he would make it his priority to return and rescue them.

They all sat, Indian and Spaniard, around the great blaze that lit up the night. Juan Hector noticed that the men who led them to this encampment were not among the group. But his thoughts quickly turned to his hunger as plates, fashioned from tree bark, and piled with items he had never seen before, were passed. But he didn't care. It was this or starve.

As they feasted, some of the men of the tribe entertained with singing or more specifically, chanting. Women began to dance before the fire, their swaying bodies casting great dark shadows against the sides of the huts. The chief who sat on a pallet, his head higher than anyone else's, clapped twice. Four young girls appeared from the shadows. Juan Hector guessed them to be no more than eleven or twelve. Each chose a Spaniard and sidled up to him. Their intent was clear, and Juan Hector would have none of it. He gently refused the approaches of the young girl who may or may not have been insulted. He could not tell. What he did know was that he could never be untrue to his Francesca. Seeing the response from their captain, the other three Spaniards reluctantly followed his example. Although, Diego, who craved female company after weeks at sea, hesitated, stroking the black, lustrous hair of his girl. She smiled seductively and moved closer. But he glanced at his captain's disapproving expression and backed away, indicating his refusal to bed with her.

At the end of the meal, a bowl filled with a strong, alcoholic brew was passed about. The chief drank first, then everyone partook. It was refilled many times. Finally, Juan Hector, sated from the meal and inebriated from the drink, excused himself and staggered to the hut that had been designated for them. He needed sleep. He was suddenly aware of his exhaustion from the events that had befallen him.

The stress of a shipwreck, the safety of his crew, and now sheltered by a tribe of Indians who may or may not look fondly on interloping Spaniards. His thoughts faded, he touched his medallion with a wish of good health and much love for his family and closed his eyes.

A few hours later, he was startled awake by men moving and loud shouts. In the dark, he felt a hand tugging at his medallion. Quickly, he leapt to his feet to see several Indians inside the hut. Carlos, Cesar, and Diego were also on their feet. In the darkness, men struggled. Cesar was able to break away to find his bag and the pistol inside.

Juan Hector kicked his way past one of the Indians and escaped out into the moonlight. He broke into a full run. He could hear footsteps following him, keeping his pace.

From behind a shot rang out, a second, and then silence. They were outnumbered.

Juan Hector kept up his speed, leaping over fallen trees, scrambling through the dense forest growth. He headed toward what appeared to be a stretch of swampy land. The moonlight glimmered on the field of sawgrass, helping him see his way. His lungs struggled; his heart pounded. The razor-sharp blades of sawgrass tore his pantaloons and scraped the skin on his legs. No one was going to take his medallion. In life or in death.

There was sudden pain. A spearhead penetrated the back of his thigh. The weapon dropping away into the grass. *It was not over*, he thought. He would just keep running. But to where? He did not have the knowledge of this land as these Indians would.

His pace faltered. He was becoming mired down by the swamp and the pain crept up and down his left leg. Another spear hit just below his right shoulder. The force pushed him forward. He lost his balance and fell, face first into the muddy water.

He could hear heavy breathing just above him. A foot kicked against his left side, and a hand gripped his left arm. He was flipped over, face upward where he could see the Indian grinning. Behind him was a dark palette of night sky, dazzling stars creating such beauty.

He knew what the Indian wanted, and he would not give it up easily. His right hand grasped the medallion more tightly than ever. The Indian reached down to take it from him, struggling to open his clutching fingers.

"Never!" Juan Hector managed to spit out. "No one will ever take this!"

Suddenly, Juan Hector heard movement, heavy splashing. In the light of a full moon, he saw it, creeping closer to him. The Indians saw it too. With one last tug, the medallion was ripped from Juan Hector's neck, and they sped away.

Moonlight sparkled from the teeth that were rapidly descending upon him. Through his fading vision he could see it was enormous. The monster, bigger than any of the ones he saw on the river, gaped once, let loose a horrifying hiss revealing the white interior of its mouth, then lunged, grabbing Juan Hector at the torso. Juan Hector could hear his rib cage snap and feel the blood spurting from his mouth. The alligator went into a spin to sever flesh. The moon and the stars disappeared, and all went black. But a moment later, Juan Hector was somehow floating above the grisly scene, watching the beast swallow his body bit by bit. Even his clothes and boots disappeared down the creature's gullet. As he watched, he felt no pain, but only a rising anger. Anger against the beast, yes, but mostly his anger targeted at the Calusa and how they had stolen his medallion and destroyed his dream of home.

The Indians jubilantly returned to the group and with head bowed, they offered the medallion to a grinning, self-satisfied chief. Once again, he had destroyed his enemy and he now held the prize to prove it.

The next day, another chain was fashioned, but not of silver but of deer skin leather, and it was ceremoniously placed over the chief's head. The air was now filled with the fetid odor of burning flesh and horrifying screams as Carlos, tied on a specially built rotisserie, slowly roasted to death. The acrid stench of sizzling flesh infected the morning air. The screaming abruptly stopped. Carlos was dead.

From the trees that edged the camps perimeter, Juan Hector watched. He didn't understand how he could be there, or how much time had passed. But he was. He watched as the tribe reveled in the slaughter. He saw Indians emerging from the boats with all the remaining goods of the Valencia. He also knew what happened to the remaining crew members he left behind. Impossibly, he could feel nothing but that anger growing within him, first of never seeing his family, at being attacked, of being devoured by a beast. How could any of this been possible?

He drifted closer to the tribe suddenly aware that he could not be seen. Yet he could see everything. He could understand their language. It was all confusing.

He heard the chief speak of how no European would usurp his power or take his land. Whoops and hollering rose up, spears were shaken in a show of unity.

The Indians who had first met Captain Juan Hector on the beach had returned, bearing pilfered sacks of yucca flour, pots, live chickens. Stolen Spanish blankets were distributed to the members of the tribe. Several fresh scalps had also been taken. No one on the beach survived, the chief was told.

Juan Hector had no sense of time. It could have been minutes, days, or weeks. But now and with great pleasure saw the onset of red oozing sores on the faces and arms of the Calusa. Burning sores festered on their tongues and soft palates. A great fatigue fell upon the tribe. Most could no longer stand with their own strength and collapsed in a heap. Women and children wailed and sobbed. What was happening to them? Many shivered pulling the pilfered blankets closer.

To Juan Hector's delight, it only got worse. They huddled in groups, wrapped in the Spanish blankets, blankets that harbored the agent of smallpox. Revenge was his!

As the chief, himself grew weary, his now sore-covered hand groped for the medallion. Perhaps, if touched, it would bring good fortune, perhaps its power would revive and save him. From the attention the Spanish captain had given it, it seemed to be of that purpose. But to his astonishment it no longer hung around his neck. He cried out to the spirits of the forest for their assistance but to no avail. It was gone. Mysteriously, inexplicably gone.

When the last of the Calusa expired, a cool wind rose from the swamps, rustling the fronds of the cat palms and giving sway to the sawgrass that clogged the waters. In the shadows, observing the inert corpses, stood a dark figure. A soft whisper floated upon the dying breeze. "*Nunca,*" it spoke. *Never.* Then like the whisper, the figure, too, vanished.

CHAPTER 13

Christine spent the morning planting the remaining trees. Once again, her son was invaluable helping her tote the pots down to the chosen spots and even jumping in to dig when Christine seemed a little tired or overheated. She'd sip from a water bottle she had placed in the freezer to chill.

"Maybe we'll find some more treasure," he said as he dug into the soil.

"And maybe not," Christine replied with a smile.

Suddenly, she realized the one thing she didn't buy was a garden hose long enough to span the distance from the house to the trees.

It didn't seem to matter as Michael looked up at the bank of dark storm clouds creeping their way.

"We'd better hurry up and finish. It looks like a storm is brewing."

Michael patted down the last of the dirt that held the lemon tree and gathered up the empty plastic containers and shovel and headed toward the house.

A jag of lightning cut the sky. The medallion, which she kept in her pocket, seemed to tingle as if it had absorbed electricity from the air.

Just as they made it to the door, the clouds opened, and the rain poured down.

"This is what to expect during the Florida summers," she told her son. "Just hope we don't get any hurricanes."

"Just a few more months for that," Michael said.

"What?" she asked.

"Hurricane season runs from June 1 to November 31," he informed her.

"Didn't know that," she said, once again outsmarted by her genius child. "Where's Maggie?"

"Dunno," he replied. "Maybe in her room watching movies."

Since her last escapade with Ben, she felt she needed to keep an eagle eye on her. She decided to go upstairs and see if she really was in her room. She crept along the hall to find her door closed. Gently, she knocked but there came no reply.

"Maggie?" she called in a soft voice. Still no response. Carefully, she turned the knob and pushed the door open. Maggie was on the bed, struggling against some unseen force. The second Christine stepped into the room, it stopped.

Maggie sat up gasping for air. "It wouldn't let me up!" she coughed. "It was choking me!"

"What was choking you?" Christine asked. "I saw nothing."

"Well, I felt it!" Her voice was returning and now she was speaking in a terrified scream. "I hate living here! I just hate it!"

"And I hate that you keep telling me that. Plain and simple, we're not moving…anywhere, so you might as well stop being a drama queen and get used to this place." She surprised herself using her son's term *drama queen* but there it was, popping out as natural as it could be. But wasn't she becoming needlessly hysterical over every little thing? Christine shut the door and headed back to the kitchen. There was no one in her closet and nothing holding her down. No Indians either. Just a huge alligator lurking beyond, in the swamp. That's what they should really worry about.

Later, after Stan had arrived home, after he had had his cocktail and after Christine had told him that the trees were finally in and they should start expecting fruit any day. "Okay, in a few months," Christine conceded. And only after the kids had left the table did she relate Maggie's experience.

"Held down?" he asked. "By what?"

"That's just it. I walked in and there was nothing except Maggie, her hands pushing something invisible away from her while she made choking sounds."

Stan thought. "Maybe this move is harder on her than we expected. Should we send her to a doctor? Maybe a therapist?"

"Not a bad idea. I'll consider it. But sure as hell, she won't like that idea."

The next morning, since it was Saturday and Stan could entertain the kids, Christine decided to go into town.

"I need a little personal time," she told him.

"Take all day!" Stan said as he kissed her and walked her to the door.

"I'm having lunch with Loretta. It's our *girls'* day."

Before meeting Loretta, Christine found the jewelry store she had researched. A nagging urge wouldn't let her rest: she needed to get a chain for the medallion.

The shop was bright and clean, unlike the coin and stamp store she had been the week before. A pretty blond greeted her from behind the counter.

She withdrew the medallion and placed it on the glass top of the display case that housed sparkling diamond rings and expensive watches.

"I'd like a chain, silver, for this."

The young lady picked it up and held it between her thumb and forefinger. It was a little larger than a silver dollar and twice as thick. But what she noticed most acutely was the strange vibration emanating from it. Immediately, she put it down.

"Let me get Danny." She disappeared for a moment returning with a tall, good-looking gentleman, his suit perfectly fitting, his black hair slicked back.

"You want a silver chain?" he asked as he picked up the medallion, quickly putting it down just as the young lady had.

Christine could tell from his expression that something about the piece made him uneasy.

"Can you do it?" she asked.

"Certainly," Danny replied. "I can have it ready by Tuesday."

"No," Christine flatly said. "It has to be now. I can't leave it."

Danny peered at Christine's hard, adamant expression. "All right," he replied.

He withdrew a red box, opened it to reveal a collection of various chains. He lifted one up and placed it next to the medallion, making certain his hand did not touch it. "It looks old," he said.

"Yes," Christine replied. "Sixteenth or seventeenth century. It's very important to me."

"Well, the silver does carry a substantial value."

"It's not the silver," she countered. "That chain looks perfect." She pointed to one still in the box as she grew anxious. She just wanted the job done. The medallion needed to be back in her possession. Then she could get on with her day.

"Good choice," Danny said. He returned the chain to the box exchanging it for Christine's choice. The links were large, so he knew it would be strong enough to support the silver's weight.

He worked quickly, not wanting the medallion to be in contact with his hands a second longer than need be. When he finished, he held it up for Christine to examine.

"It's perfect," she said, maybe a little too tersely. "What do I owe you?

As Danny ran her credit card for the $75 chain, she slipped it over her head. The medallion, for the first time in over four hundred years, hung from a neck. She touched it and felt its vibration become stronger, if that was at all possible. The jewelry shop's temperature seemed to drop dramatically. Even Danny felt it.

He returned the credit card to Christine, who without so much as a thank you or goodbye, spun around and left.

"She was an odd one," he said to his blond assistant, who reappeared from the back room. "Take a look at the thermostat. It just got cold in here."

Christine was right on time. Loretta arrived at the door of the restaurant at precisely the same moment. They exchanged hugs and cheek kisses and went inside. As they were seated, the waiter who had served them before, the same one Christine had snapped at, leaned over to his colleague. "They're back! Ladies from Hell!"

"You have to see," Christine practically squealed as she withdrew the medallion from her blouse. "I put it on a chain."

"Very nice," Loretta felt compelled to say. "But isn't it a little heavy?"

"Not at all! I love it. This way, I can have it with me all the time."

Loretta picked up the menu, then glanced up to see approaching them the same waiter as before. "Now be nice," she whispered.

Christine didn't understand until the server appeared.

"I'll be nice," she promised. She turned her attention back to the young man. "Bring us a bottle of that chardonnay we had last time. Please."

Loretta broke into a broad smile. "Much better. So what's going on with you?"

Christine sighed. "Maggie. She said there was a man who came out of her closet and yesterday, I walked into her room and she was on the bed, struggling against some invisible force. It stopped the minute my foot hit the floor."

"What do you think is going on?"

Christine's head tilted to one side. "Don't know. I spoke to Stan and we think maybe the move down here hit her harder than we anticipated. Maybe a therapist."

Loretta couldn't help but notice how Christine's left hand had migrated to the medallion and how her fingers folded tightly around the silver. It seemed an unconscious movement.

"Maybe I can help you find some good doctors. God knows, in this town therapists are as common as wine."

The waiter uncorked the bottle and filled their glasses.

They clinked. "Here's to friendship and wine." They took sips and set the glasses back down.

"I finally planted all the trees. Thank God for Michael's help."

"Is he having any weird experiences?" Loretta asked.

Christine stopped to think. "He reported what he called a shadow man in his room one night."

"Shadow man? What's that?"

Christine shrugged. "He said it looked like a large man but as a shadow so black that it he couldn't see the wall behind it."

"Did it threaten him?"

With a shake of her head, she replied that Michael didn't seem to be threatened. "In fact, he went right back to his room and went to sleep."

Loretta couldn't help considering what Matty had been telling her. But haunted houses were only the stuff of movies and wild imaginations. That can of worms kept taunting her. Yet Christine had been reporting too many inexplicable events occurring at the house and as she debated between a Caesar salad or a turkey club, she came up with an idea, one she would keep to herself until the time was right.

Loretta arrived home to find Matty in his usual position, wineglass in reach and the television flickering another one of his frivolous shows.

She set her purse down and faced him.

"What's up?" Matty asked.

"I'm not sure," she replied. "Maybe you can actually be of some help."

Matty quieted the television with the remote. "Really? This should be good."

"Don't get all snarky on me."

"All right. What can I help you with?"

"I want to find someone who can put an end to all this crazy stuff at Hawk's Bend."

Matty sat up. "So you believe?"

"No! Not at all. But maybe a third party can help. Christine has been telling me about the goings-on over there. I think it's all her imagination."

Matty thought for a moment. "How about a medium?"

"A what?"

"A psychic medium."

"How do you know anything about that?"

He glanced over at the TV. "Believe it or not, I actually learn stuff from that thing. Those shows about the paranormal. They bring in a medium who can sense what's going on."

"And where would I find one of those?" Loretta asked, shaking her head in a way that Matty couldn't quite interpret.

"Call a paranormal group. You should be able to find one online."

Loretta said nothing more. She sat at the kitchen table with her laptop and began the search, wondering if she wouldn't be better off just keeping out of it. But Christine was a friend and needed help, even if it was to dispel the imaginings of her daughter and herself.

Almost immediately, Loretta found a group. The Florida West Coast Paranormal Investigators. She copied down the phone number, closed her laptop, and called.

Misty answered the phone. Loretta had hit pay dirt. After a short conversation, Misty gave the name and number of a woman the team often works with.

"She's amazing," Misty told her. "If anyone can help, it would be Diane. And," she added, "if necessary we can send our group and do a full investigation."

Loretta thanked her and dialed Diane's number.

*****

Christine drove slowly up to her house. That's when she heard it. A voice. Low and soft. She peered in the rearview mirror. She was alone. It spoke again but she could barely make out the words. What was happening, she wondered. Was she going crazy? Then it stopped. Maybe a little more wine would help, she thought as she made her way to the kitchen, opened the fridge door and found a fresh bottle.

Everything was so quiet. She wondered where Stan and the kids might be.

After she poured a glass, she moved to the windows overlooking the yard. There they were, out on the lawn playing badminton. For a while, she just stood, sipping chardonnay, gazing out at her family rushing back and forth, chasing some silly shuttlecock.

Then she froze. Standing just within the shadows of the trees— it was them. Two of them, dark and amorphous. She could see right through them to the vegetation behind.

But instead of fearing them, she grew angry. Not an anger against strangers trespassing on their property but some other anger, an older one. She clutched the medallion and went out to the pool.

Stan was a one-man team against the two kids. But she wasn't watching them, she was staring at the uninvited guests, who now stared directly back at her.

They could see her, she knew. Suddenly, she whispered the word *never. Where did that come from?* she thought.

She crossed the lawn, bypassing the playing field and headed directly toward the two dark shadows who seemed to be waiting for her.

"Never!" she said aloud. "NEVER!"

Stan came up from behind. "Why are you screaming? Who are you screaming at?"

Christine turned and looked him in the face, her eyes like blackened coals, her cheeks flushed.

Stan jumped back. Her face became so contorted that she little resembled his wife. "Christine!" He moved back to her and grabbed her shoulders. "Christine! What's going on?"

Slowly her senses returned, the blue of her eyes reappeared, her face relaxed, and the anger subsided.

She turned pointing back to the trees. "They were there. Calusa."

Michael and Maggie had joined their parents.

"Calusa?" Michael blurted. "How would you know that, Mom?"

Christine stared blankly at them.

"Mom, they were a tribe from hundreds of years ago. They're extinct."

Stan put his arm around her, gently guiding her back to the house. "You need a glass of wine."

The kids watched as they disappeared inside.

"Told you," Maggie said. "There's something weird about this place."

"I've seen them, too," Michael confessed.

Maggie wanted to tell her brother that she, too, saw strange men in the trees. It was the day of the alligator attack. But she decided against it. She would just be accused of whining.

Once settled at the kitchen table, Stan refilled the glass she had already started. Then he noticed the medallion.

"You put it on a chain?"

She looked down at it, felt its tingling and touched it with the fingers of her left hand. "Today. Before lunch with Loretta."

"But why?" he asked. "It's not really your taste in jewelry."

With a bewildered glance first at him and then to her wine glass, she said, "But I love it. I found it. It's mine. It's my treasure."

Stan shrugged. "Fine with me."

Suddenly, she snarled. "It's mine. No one will ever take it. Never!"

Stan stepped back, away from the table, away from Christine. "Honey, calm down. No one will ever take it from you. I promise."

This seemed to appease her.

"I'll be out in the garage," Stan said. He left her at the table to drink her wine as he began to question her emotional state. Their focus had been on Maggie, but maybe Christine was going through something, too, but was just better at hiding it. Now that he'd have more time at home, he promised himself that he was going to keep a close eye on her.

CHAPTER 14

Wednesday morning Christine received an unexpected call from Loretta. She asked if she could bring a friend over to see the house. The woman was visiting from out of town, Loretta had said.

Christine was happy to have the company. "I'll make lunch," she offered.

Loretta objected. "We'll stop at the deli on Atlantic Avenue and pick up sandwiches. You're not going to fuss."

"What about wine?" Christine asked.

"Yes, you can fuss with the wine."

They arrived at one p.m. As promised, Loretta toted a large brown bag loaded with sandwiches, chips, and pickles.

Christine met them at the door, ushering them inside. But Loretta's friend paused. "Mind if I just take in the front of the house? It's quite palatial."

Loretta stepped past Christine and entered the house. "She called me out of the blue. We haven't seen each other in years."

"What's her name?"

"Oh, Diane. She's very nice."

They heard the front door reopen, then close, and Diane appeared at the kitchen door. She was a bit portly, clad in a button-down plaid shirt, jeans, and hiking boots, her mousy brown hair was streaked with gray and pulled back in a ponytail. Her eyes were dark brown, and she peered around with an intensity that took Christine off-guard.

Something, a feeling, began to stir in Christine. It was not a good feeling. She wasn't sure if she was going to like Diane. But for Loretta's sake, she would keep her feelings in check.

"Diane, this is Christine." Loretta said.

Diane extended her meaty hand and touched Christine's. "Very beautiful," she said, referring to the house.

"Thanks. I owe it all to Loretta. She's the one who showed it to me."

Christine busied herself emptying the bag of its contents onto the kitchen table. She brought down plates from the cabinet and knives and forks from the drawer. Of course, glasses for the wine she had been chilling.

"Some chardonnay, Diane?"

Diane smiled. "No, thanks. I don't drink."

Christine glanced over at Loretta who could only shrug.

"Do you mind if I look around?"

"Not at all. Please make yourself at home."

Diane noticed that the table was pretty much ready for diners. "Go ahead and eat. I'm really not that hungry."

They watched as she moved deeper into the house, disappearing altogether.

"She's a little odd," Christine said, popping a potato chip into her mouth.

"Yeah, I guess she is a little. But aren't we all?"

"How do you know her?"

Loretta tried to remember the story she and Diane had concocted, that they had been in college together and shared a dorm room for a couple semesters, until Diane transferred to another school. They found each other again on social media.

Diane had been gone for quite a while. But it didn't deter Loretta and Christine from chugging down more wine. Christine leaned in closer to Loretta.

"I don't want anyone to overhear us," Christine whispered.

Loretta pulled her chair up to the table, curious as to what big secret Christine was going to share.

"He bought a gun."

Loretta's eyes grew wide. "Stan? But why?"

"He says he'd feel better since the house is so isolated. I didn't like the idea one bit. And the kids know nothing about it."

"Well, maybe it's not such a bad idea." Loretta spoke quietly and quickly in case Diane returned.

Christine suddenly spotted her, out on the lawn, standing by the newly planted fruit trees. From there she strolled farther down, toward the swamp.

"Hope that alligator doesn't make a show," Christine said, half smirking. "But I have a gun now!"

Diane turned her back to the swamp and took a long, concentrated gaze back to the house.

"What in the world is she doing?"

Loretta shook her head. "I think she's an artist now. Maybe she's just taking it all in."

By the time they had finished their lunch, Diane returned. She stepped up to Christine and pointed to the medallion, though it was hidden beneath her blouse where only someone with x-ray vision could see it.

"May I see?" Diane asked.

Christine glanced at Loretta, then withdrew the medallion.

Diane placed a finger on the silver. "It feels like it's alive."

Jealously, Christine slipped it back beneath her blouse. "It's mine," she said for no apparent reason.

"Yes," Diane said. "It is yours." She looked at her watch and turned to Loretta. "Do you mind? It's getting late and I have a few things I have to do."

"Not at all," Loretta replied. She began to gather up plates, but Christine stopped her. "No, I'll do it. You've done enough."

She escorted them to the door, where she hugged Loretta, and shook Diane's hand again. "It was very nice meeting you."

"Likewise," Diane said.

They headed down the porch steps to the car. In a second, they disappeared down the road.

Once away from the house, Loretta took a deep breath. "So everything is just as I said it was. Right?"

Diane's expression changed to worry. "No."

"What do you mean?"

"There's a dark and dangerous energy not only in that house but on the land."

Loretta began to regret executing the great idea she had had at lunch. After some quick researching, she found Diane, a psychic medium. Under false pretenses, she would take her to the house on Hawk's Bend and prove, once and for all, that nothing unusual or paranormal was going on. Boy, she had anticipated with great satisfaction the I-told-you-so she would drop on the lap of her lazy-ass husband Matty. Now what?

"It's an old energy. I would even guess it's taken on a demonic form."

"Demonic?" Loretta repeated. "This is over my head."

"But it's not just one. There are several. On the property. It's almost as if there is a struggle going on." Diane looked straight ahead at the ribbon of road as she explained. "It's difficult to fully understand. Not with the little time I had. But usually, these forces create havoc on the living. They attempt to cause disruption. They even try to convince the weak ones to kill themselves or someone else. It's a way of replenishing their waning energy. Regardless, your friend and her family could be in serious danger." After a short silence Diane added, "The house should be cleansed."

"Cleansed?" Loretta was having a difficult time digesting all what Diane was telling her.

"Spiritually cleansed," Diane clarified. "And that medallion. It's the nexus for everything evil."

Loretta dropped Diane at the spot where she had parked her car, at the real estate office. She thanked her profusely.

"You have my number," Diane said. "Please call me, and we'll arrange for a time that I can return and perform that cleansing. We may even have to do an exorcism of the house."

Loretta waited until Diane's car had left the parking lot. *Exorcism! Can it be that bad?* she wondered. This was getting more serious, more complicated, more dangerous than she could have ever dreamed.

Then she considered what she had done, lying to her friend, introducing Diane under false pretenses. Now she had shocking information. How could she tell Christine? If she did, Christine would know about the ruse and hate her forever. But if Diane was right that the Minters were in danger, something had to be done. *A no-win situation*, Loretta conceded. And now she had to tell Matty that his friends were right. The house was haunted. That was the part that bothered her the most.

Chapter 15

Christine was pouring her first cup of coffee of the day when she heard a knock on the door. It wasn't quite like the other knocks she had heard throughout the house since moving in. It just seemed a little different. Maybe it was from someone real.

She opened the door to find Ben, beguiling in tight shorts, a blue tank top, and sunglasses that made him look like a celebrity.

"Come in," Christine said, wondering why he was there in the first place.

"Is Maggie ready?"

"Ready? Ready for what?" she asked.

"We're meeting my mom at the mall."

"Really?" She wondered if he was telling her the truth. Then a strange sensation invaded her. Her facial features softened, and she said, "I think she's upstairs." Unexpectedly, her hand brushed across his forehead, sweeping the lock of hair that had fallen just above his eyes. Then she gently touched his left arm with an imperceptible squeeze of his bicep. "You work out a lot?"

Uncomfortably, he moved back, toward the closed front door.

"I try," he replied, relieved to see Maggie standing at the top of the stairs, staring down at them, aghast at what her mother was doing.

"Mother!" she shouted as she ran down the steps. "Get away from him."

Christine spun around. "What's the matter?"

"You're flirting with Ben."

"Oh, please. Such an imagination."

Ben turned, opened the door, and stepped out onto the porch. "Let's go," he called. "My Ma will be waiting."

Maggie flashed Christine a look of disgust and pushed passed her, slamming shut the door with a loud bang.

For a few minutes, Christine just stood, staring at the door, squeezing her medallion, wondering what had just happened. Did she really flirt with a seventeen-year-old boy? *Impossible*, she thought, not quite remembering the last minutes before he and her daughter stomped away. It was as if something had taken over her body and mind.

That's when the whispering began. It was the same voice she had heard before. She spun around expecting to see someone in the foyer with her. But there was no one. She must be going crazy! The voice must be coming from inside her head. Isn't that one of the first signs of insanity?

She returned to the kitchen and retrieved the coffee cup. It wasn't like her, harassing a child and now angering her daughter. And hearing voices on top of it.

She took the coffee and went out to the pool. The morning was a little cloudy, with sunshine breaking through at intervals. Wondering how her trees were doing, she made a trip across the lawn to where her little grove was clustered. The orange blossoms were beginning to open, emitting a most exotically sweet and hypnotic aroma. Buds were forming on the lime and lemon trees, while the others were not yet showing their abilities. Quietly, she stood admiring her work when a wave of anger overwhelmed her. Her hand went immediately to the medallion, and she spun around to see the forms of three Calusa standing among the cabbage palms and myrtles. They were staring directly at her. A cold shiver ran through her, but it did nothing to mitigate the rising fury.

"Never!" she screamed at them. The voice rising from her wasn't hers. It was deeper, and very angry. "It's mine!"

They ignored her outburst and began to advance. Her free hand began to touch the pockets of her jeans. The gun wasn't there. She had left it in the bedroom closet.

The three figures continued to move closer, gliding through the foliage and across the lawn as though by levitation.

"It's mine!" she screamed again, holding the medallion as well as her ground. They didn't scare her. They only infuriated her.

When they had come as close as ten feet from her, they magically faded, disappearing altogether.

Her anger began to fade also, quickly dissipating as the Calusa did, and as quickly as it came upon her.

What did they want? she asked herself, quickly returning to the patio, surprised that she had no fear of them, only fury. Spinning on her heels, peering back down the lawn to make certain they were gone. Suddenly, she knew the answer to her query. The medallion. They wanted the medallion. But she had no intention of giving it up. She had found it, she had put a chain on it—it was hers. No one was going to take it from her. No one. Never would she give it up. Never!

When Stan arrived home in time for dinner, he accepted the drink she had poured for him, and asked how her day had been.

At first, she considered telling him about her unexpected meeting out on the lawn with the Indians, but instead, she told him how her trees were coming along and how they might have fresh fruit sooner than expected. Then she mentioned that Maggie had gone to the mall with Ben.

"I thought they were to be chaperoned." He sipped vodka.

"Ben told me they were meeting his mother there."

"And you believed him?"

Just then Maggie entered the kitchen. "And did you tell Dad how you were coming on to Ben?"

Stan set his drink down. "What?"

"Oh, please," Christine said. "I did nothing of the sort. I would never do anything like that. He's just a boy."

"I saw you!" Maggie countered. "Ben told me."

Michael stepped into the room and took his place at the table. "What's all the yelling about?" he asked.

Stan picked up his glass again. "Nothing. Just a little miscommunication."

Christine retrieved a bottle of wine from the refrigerator and poured a glass for herself. She noticed her hand trembling. *The lying bitch,* she thought. *I would never do such a thing.* And if she had, she couldn't remember any of it. With a gulp, she emptied half the glass, then refilled it. "Everyone! Sit down. Dinner is ready."

Stan gestured for Maggie to take her place, but she refused. "I'm not hungry. I'm going to my room."

They watched her storm away, stomping as loudly as she could up the staircase.

"What's wrong with her?" Michael asked.

"Nothing," Stan replied. "Just eat."

After dinner, after the kitchen was cleaned, Stan and Christine took seats by the pool.

"So?"

"So what?" Christine replied.

"What happened with Ben?"

"Nothing," Christine said in a heavy whisper. "I'm a schoolteacher. I could never touch a child." She gazed up at the night sky that had finally cleared completely, noticing how bright the stars shone. "Maggie is going through a stage. She's more than likely mad at me for the limitations I placed on her as far as that boy goes."

"I suppose," Stan agreed.

A sound distracted them from their conversation. At first, they thought it was the barn owl that often broke the evening silence with its eerie hooting, but this wasn't that. It came from where her trees were planted. At first a mournful sound, then a sound of what seemed to be a sharp cry.

Her hand held tightly to the medallion. Maybe it was the Calusa returning. They were hunting her; she could feel it. She was about to tell Stan about her morning experience but another cry, much like a man in great pain, broke the silence, and then faded away. Her mind changed; he would never hear about it. Never.

Chapter 16

Ever since Diane had visited, the energy in the house seemed to intensify to almost palpable levels. Things went missing more often, a shoe, a watch; scratching could be heard inside the walls—more than likely rodents, Christine believed. Footsteps were being heard late at night, on the staircase, in the upper hallway. Sometimes it would wake everyone up. Michael, visibly shaken, would appear at their door, asking if he could sleep in their room. Stan would always allow it, but he would have to sleep on the floor. He was too old to be sleeping in their bed. Maggie would sometimes scream in the middle of the night. Stan would hurry down to find her sitting upright on her bed, mumbling about shadows and bed shakings. For everyone, sleep was becoming a rare commodity, and everyone's nerves were becoming raw.

"We've got to do something," Stan finally said as he finished his coffee, and headed for the door.

"Do what? I'll call the Gator Boys, maybe they can figure a way to get the mice out of the walls."

"Mice?"

Stan realized that for the first time he was beginning to believe that something paranormal was going on. He could not rationalize the events taking place, and as much as he was a skeptic, he found himself, slowly becoming a believer. But what it was, he had no clue.

"All that scratching. It's gotta be mice or squirrels or something."

Stan stared at her incredulously. He was beginning to think his wife was not only in a state of denial, but that there was something beyond rational explanations happening in the house.

"Forget the Gator Boys, find a priest." With that he was gone, headed for the hotel.

"Priest?" Christine said after he had left. "How's that going to help?"

She finished her coffee and went upstairs to find Michael in Maggie's room. They were staring at the television. A nature show was on, something about sea life, sharks, and whales.

Michael looked up at his mother. "Maggie asked me if I would keep her company."

"Why? You two never get along."

"There were some creepy sounds in my room too."

"Too?" Christine asked.

"There's creepy sounds everywhere in this house," Michael said.

"I hate this house," Maggie suddenly snarled.

Michael looked over at her, surprised at the strangeness of her voice.

"Once, again," Christine said, "We all know how you feel about this house, but we're here to stay."

Michael looked at his mother. "Do you ever take that off," he asked referring to the medallion hanging around her neck.

"Never!" she replied, her voice rising in decibels. With that, she hastily retreated from the room, leaving the kids to their show.

"I hate her," Maggie admitted to her brother.

"Don't say that," Michael implored then fell to a moment of thought. "But she is getting a little weird since we moved here."

"Weird isn't the word," his sister said. They turned their attention back to the television to see an orca attacking a sea lion.

CHAPTER 17

Stan found Loretta waiting for him at the hotel's bar. He thought it odd that she had called him to arrange a meeting. Loretta was Christine's friend, why call him?

Regardless of the early hour, Loretta had ordered a glass of wine and had finished half of it by the time Stan saw her. She looked a little frazzled and her hand trembled noticeably.

"Loretta," he said greeting her with one of his beaming smiles.

"Hi, Stan. Thanks for seeing me." She marveled at how crystal blue his eyes shown in the bright sunlight that blazed through the windowpanes.

"Anytime. You're a friend."

She downed the rest of the wine and asked if they could speak privately.

Stan led her to the hostess podium and informed the girl behind it that they would take a table in the back of the room for a quiet chat. "And please ask a server to bring another glass of wine for the lady."

They settled in at an out of the way table.

"What's going on?" Stan asked straightforwardly.

A glass of wine appeared; Stan thanked the server then turned his attention back to Loretta.

"I didn't know what else to do," she said. "I couldn't talk to Christine about what I've done, but I couldn't ignore it."

"What are you talking about?" Stan pressed, confused. His smile had faded, and his features settled into an expression of concern.

Loretta took a sip from the refreshed glass. "Well, every time I meet with her, she tells me about the weird goings-on in your house, about the kids having a hard time being there, especially Maggie. And that medallion. She clings to it like a lifeline."

Stan nodded. "Things have been a bit strange. At first, I wasn't sure. But now I think something paranormal might be going on."

"It's affecting Christine. I didn't want to believe it either, but my husband kept insisting that your house might be haunted. His buddies believe the same thing."

Stan sat quietly trying to digest everything he was being told. He didn't want to admit it, but Christine was changing. She was transforming into a bitter and angry woman. It was a fact he could no longer deny.

"But it gets worse," Loretta added.

Stan steeled himself. "Worse?"

"I did something dishonest." Loretta took in a deep breath. "I called in a psychic medium. Diane. I introduced her to Christine as an old friend, but I just wanted her to get a feel of the house, to hopefully debunk everything as imagination."

"And?"

She took another sip of wine. "She said things weren't good."

"What do you mean?"

"She said a sort of paranormal struggle was going on. And she called the medallion a nexus of evil. It seemed to be generating all the activity. She said the house should be cleansed."

"What do you mean—cleansed?"

"Spiritually. I wasn't sure what she meant either. But that's what she said."

A sense of relief surged through Loretta's body. There, she said it. She got it out of her system.

A silence settled over the two of them until Stan spoke: "Just before I left this morning, I told Christine to find a priest. She looked at me like I was crazy. My guess is she won't. Can this Diane be of any help?"

"I have her number," Loretta said. "I'll call her."

"Thanks," Stan said glancing at his watch, realizing he was running late for a meeting. "Hey, I gotta go. Enjoy the wine and if you'd like another just ask the bartender. My treat."

Loretta offered a weak smile of thanks and then her expression turned to panic. "Don't say anything to Christine. Please! I don't want her to get angry with me and break up our friendship."

"It's just between us," he assured her as he began to maneuver though the dining room tables finally disappearing into the lobby.

*****

Christine wandered back out to her fruit trees. More buds were sprouting, an indication of a good crop. But it didn't seem to please her. As she stood staring at the new growth a slight breeze wafted across her. It seemed to be coming from the direction of the swamp. Then she heard or thought she heard it—that voice, low and guttural, like a growl: "Do it!"

"Do it?" she repeated aloud.

"Do it!" The breeze faded as did the voice.

She spun around, thinking someone was nearby playing with her. But there was nothing except grass, shrubs, and palms. She slowly wandered closer to the barrier that hid the muddy waters beyond, to get a better look at what was called the Everglades, or at least the western part of it. She could see the thick sawgrass sprouting from dark waters and as she drew closer, pushing branches out of her way, and bending fronds to get a better look, she saw it. The gator! It lazed peacefully in the water, it's snout and eyes exposed, the scales of its long tail appearing like rivets along the surface. Surprisingly, it instilled no fear in her. It was acting quite docile and nonthreatening.

But then she saw something else. It was a Calusa, standing just beyond the reptile. A spear grasped in one hand, its dark eyes focused first on the gator, then lifting, directly on to her. A chill shuddered her body. Unlike the gator, he appeared very threatening. She could clearly see the pock marks that covered his face, his hands, and legs. It reached out an arm to her, its right index finger, pointing at her, indicating something. What?

But she knew, of course. Instinctively. Unconsciously. It wanted her medallion. Her eyes narrowed. "Never!" she screamed into the emptiness of the swamp. The power of her angry voice frightening a pair of roosting egrets from the tree above her head. The gator stirred, adjusting its body so that it now faced her directly.

The Indian approached. It didn't wade through the water like a normal flesh and blood man might but incredibly, floated above the surface as if by magic, defying the laws of gravity and nature.

"Never!" she screamed again as she watched the specter approach. The gator, with a swirl of its muscular tail and a thunderous splash, disappeared deeper into the swamps.

Her fingers tightened onto the medallion, and she began to run back toward the house, driven by the anger growing inside her, an anger aimed at anyone who tried to steal her medallion, even at an imagined Calusa. An anger that, day by day, gradually increased. An anger she did not understand yet could not quell.

When she got to the patio, she stopped to catch her breath. Spinning around, it was clear the thing was no longer in pursuit, but she waited a few moments all the same, if for no other reason than to let her heartbeat return to normal.

The voice returned: "You know what you have to do."

She could see no one. Was the voice in her own head, she wondered. Was she going crazy? Her hands flew up to cover her ears. "Stop!" she screamed. She then wondered, what did it mean, "Do it"? Do what?

Her breathing was slowing. What she needed was a glass of wine.

When she entered the kitchen, all the cabinet doors were once again opened although nothing had been pulled out and strewn. She released an audible sigh of disgust. Slammed a few doors then looked up at the ceiling. "What the fuck do you want?"

She wondered why she even asked the question. It was the medallion.

Maggie appeared at the kitchen door. "Who are you talking to?"

Christine ignored the question, slammed shut the last remaining cabinet door and retrieved the bottle of wine from the refrigerator.

"Aren't you drinking a lot, Mom? It's only eleven a.m."

The bottle slammed onto the tabletop. "Why don't you just mind your own business!"

Maggie stepped back, shocked by her mother's voice.

The ring of Christine's cell phone broke the tension. It was Stan.

"Being Friday, I'm leaving early. Tell the kids that we're going to the movies."

"Fine!" Christine snarled into the phone, then disconnected the call. Without taking her gaze from the glass, she repeated what Stan had said.

Maggie smiled for the first time in a while, happy that she'd spend time not only away from the house but with her father. She sped upstairs to give her brother the news and help decide which film they should see.

Christine was ready to pour a second glass when her phone rang again. It was Loretta, reminding Christine of their luncheon date the next day.

"I'll be there," Christine replied a bit lethargically. "Can't wait."

It was about two when Stan got home. He found Christine sitting by the pool, drinking more wine.

"Hi, sweetie!" His voice was cheerful. He bent down and placed a kiss on her cheek. "Everything okay? Did you have a nice day?"

She barely moved her head to look at him. "Yeah, everything was great." She responded without any emotion. "Trees are doing great."

Stan wanted to comment on her lackadaisical, if not apathetic tone of voice, but he held back. It would only be a start of an argument. Instead, he asked if she wanted to go to the movies with them.

"No," she replied.

"We'll go out to dinner afterward," he added as bait.

"No. You and the kids go. I'm tired."

"You sure?"

"Yeah. Have fun," she said in a flat monotone.

"Okay."

Stan disappeared into the house wondering why his wife looked almost comatose, or maybe in a trance. Maybe the house was affecting her, or more precisely whatever was going on inside the house. That Diane friend of Loretta's should be able to help. He would have to hope. But his optimism was short lived when Loretta called him.

Unfortunately, Diane was busy until the following weekend. They would have to wait another week, suffer through another seven days of unexplained activity, and probably another week of Christine's disagreeable mood.

The kids stumbled down the stairs when they heard their father's voice. It seemed like Christmas with the gift being their father. A few minutes later, they were packed into the car, heading for the Strand Theater.

Christine, meanwhile, remained outside at the patio, despite the heat. Sweat began to bead along her upper lip but she didn't seem to notice.

The sun was slowly drifting westward, and long shadows crawled across the lawn. Another one appeared down by the swamp. Just staring up at the house, up at Christine. Again, her fingers tightened around the medallion. She rose out of her chair and stared back.

"Never!" she shouted. "Never! I'll die first!"

Instead of dinner, Christine substituted yet another glass of wine. She was on a second bottle, secretly determined to finish it too. Climbing the staircase, she headed for the bedroom. She plopped onto the edge of her bed, glass in hand, bottle on the nightstand pondering the day's events. The whereabouts of her husband and children didn't once enter her mind. Thoughts of them were too upsetting, irritating as though they had become the bane of her existence. They wanted her medallion, too, she convinced herself. No one was safe. No one could be trusted. Dark thoughts.

The phone rang, and she could see it was her mother. Fifth time this week her mother called, and the fifth time Christine ignored it. *Probably just wants a freebie week down here. Doesn't she have a life?* Christine thought.

The room became suddenly chilly. A coldness that caused a shiver. She could see her breath. Then in front of her, against the wall a dark amorphous shape appeared, like a dense black cloud that light could not penetrate. It began to organize until it took the shape of a man. Astonished, Christine could only look on helplessly. Bit by bit, she could start making out the eyes, dark, cold, and cruel, short black curly hair, a scruffy, bearded face, an odd uniform that seemed to be

Spanish, or at least that's what she remembered from one of her son's Florida history books. His shirt was bloodstained and torn. Her eyes dropped to the floor to see that whatever this was had no feet, his pantaloons fading at the ankles.

The figure scowled. "Do it!" it said.

It was the same voice she had heard earlier. The voice she thought was coming from inside her head. Now she knew it was *his* voice.

"Do what?" she asked, angry and frustrated. Her voice rose, "Do what?"

"You know!" With that, it faded completely away. She was convinced her imagination was now on overdrive. None of any of this was happening, not the noises, not the tapping, not the menacing Calusa or dark Spaniard. Nothing. She was going crazy, she thought. Was she?

She laid back against the pillow, finishing the wine in her glass and setting it next to the half-filled bottle. She wasn't going to finish it off after all. Sleep fell over her so deeply that she didn't notice Stan climbing under the sheets beside her or the scratching inside the wall that kept Stan awake until it stopped as mysteriously as it started.

⎯⎯◯⎯⎯

Chapter 18

It was three a.m. when Christine awoke from a sound sleep. Reaching for the medallion, she was relieved it was still hanging on her neck. It was the dream that aroused her. Stan and the kids were trying to wrestle her medallion away from her. There was a struggle. The three of them conspired against her. They attacked her at every angle, reaching for the chain, grabbing at her medallion. Their faces were contorted, monstrous. She fought and struggled until she saw an escape. She pulled away, medallion intact, and ran for her life, knowing that they would kill her. Her own family! They would kill her.

She sat up, astounded that her own loved ones would do such a thing, to collude, to plan such an assault. Didn't they know the importance of the medallion? In her mind, it was no longer a dream, but reality. There no longer was a boundary between dream and reality. The anger built. Hatred grew. How could they do such a thing? Did they have no respect? She heard the voice again. The voice respected her. It drove her. It commanded her. The voice was the only thing she could now trust. And she listened.

Quietly, gently she pulled the covers off. She did not want to wake Stan. Her body seethed with hatred. Hatred for everyone and everything. It was a feeling she was unaccustomed to, yet it felt perfectly natural. She stood and looked back at the bed. Stan snored gently; his black hair tousled across the white pillowcase. She felt nothing for him. It was as if a stranger slept beside her.

Turning her back from her husband, she instinctively went to the closet. There she moved her hand under the winter clothes that were stored upon the highest shelf. Her hand slid beneath the cardigans and woolens until she found it. Her breath quickened. It was like finding a gift under the tree on Christmas morning.

Slowly, she extracted the weapon and for a moment held it in her right hand. The metal was cold, but not as cold as the room had become. The temperature had dropped quickly.

"*Nunque.*" She heard it. Though in Spanish, she instinctively knew what it meant. She was no longer herself. She was the rightful owner of the medallion that hung from her neck, that bounced against her breasts as she moved. The voice of the Spaniard resonated in her brain. "Do it," he kept repeating. Her body trembled. It felt like someone or something was entering her, absorbed by the pores of her skin. It made her feel strong. And furious.

Of course, she would do it. Everyone was her enemy. Everyone wanted to steal the medallion from her. Didn't they know how important it was? Didn't they know that it once harbored all her love? Now it resonated all her hate. Hate for anyone who might want to take it from her.

Leveling the gun, she took aim at Stan. He slept on his right side, his back to her, quietly breathing. His handsome features had become hideous. A freak. Looking at him nauseated her. But it would soon end. He would never take the medallion from her.

She lifted the pistol, took aim, and shot. The bullet struck Stan's head, penetrating the brain. The force shattered skull bone. She heard it, pleased by the sound. Blood slowly dribbled onto the pillow case. His thick black hair turned a dark crimson. His breathing ceased.

Satisfied that she had rid herself of one of her enemies, she proceeded out of the room and stealthily headed down the hall. The second enemy needed to be engaged. Michael.

Mr. Know-It-All, she thought as she stood for a moment to stare at him, blissfully sleeping, and unaware that he had become prey for a remorseless and ruthless monster. And Christine had become a monster. Her skin crawled with the evil that now existed inside her, that now controlled her every thought, every emotion, every move.

Her lips curled into a contemptuous smile, the gun now pointed at his skull. He wouldn't take the medallion from her either, not like he did out on the lawn the day she found it. He was secretly plotting to take it from her. She couldn't allow that. It had to come to an end.

She lifted the gun, aiming at the boy, quickly pulled the trigger. The recoil pushed her off balance, but she caught herself on a desk.

The thing inside her seemed to now be experiencing a joyful victory. Gaining renewed energy with each kill. One step closer to its goal.

The voice told her to hurry.

She left Michael's shattered corpse, blood drooling from the corners of his mouth, staining the pillowcase, pooling onto the sheets.

Driven by the voice, she quickly found her way to Maggie's bedroom. The door was closed, but not locked. Quietly, she nudged it open with her right foot. The girl slept fitfully. Arms twitched, a foot made a small kick against the comforter.

"Little slut," Christine whispered.

Maggie must have heard Christine's voice. Her eyes fluttered open to find her mother standing over her. But her face was contorted into an evil mask. Maggie could barely recognize her. But she did recognize that she held a pistol. Something that should never have been in her mother's hand. She began to cry out, but her voice was drowned out by the pop of the bullet. Her forehead cracked open, and the room went black.

Christine watched jubilantly as the girl's head slip to one side. It was done. Her enemies had been vanquished.

But the evil thing inside of her had yet finished.

Calmly, for the thing itself found a moment of calm, but growing strength. This evil fed on life forces and it had been hungry for too long.

Christine left the room, returning to the master bedroom. Without so much as a peek at her dead husband, she grabbed what was left of the wine and went downstairs to the kitchen.

Taking a seat at the table, she upended the bottle and chugged down a generous mouthful of Chardonnay.

He appeared, that Spaniard. His body seemed less amorphous this time, more solid, more tangible. There was a sardonic grin on his bearded face. And for the first time, she could see his feet, small, booted, and laced.

At first, his dark, lifeless eyes focused hungrily upon the medallion swinging from her neck. Then he turned his head to gaze far out to the swamps. Out there his remains lay buried under centuries of accumulated muck, gone and forgotten. His rage grew more intensely. He had almost forgotten what had happened to his earthly self until his gaze shifted back to the medallion. The memories came rushing back. Those cruel and greedy heathens that not only took his life but also stole the one precious thing. And they were still there, plotting on taking it back. He couldn't allow such a thing. He needed more energy to fuel his existence.

"Do it," he whispered.

Christine felt the force of his voice, more now than all the times before when he spoke to her.

She took another mouthful of wine, felt numbness slowly overtaking her body. Obediently, she lifted the gun from the table top and pushed the muzzle deep into her mouth. Without a second of hesitation, she pulled the trigger.

And the Spaniard surged with renewed power.

*****

Loretta had waited a half hour at the restaurant before she started calling Christine. After a few attempts, she became worried. She paid for the wine she had consumed, left the restaurant, got into her car, heading to Hawk's Bend.

She couldn't understand why Christine would miss their lunch. She was also too responsible to not call if she had to cancel. But as she neared the house, a creeping feeling began in her gut. *Something wasn't right*, she thought. She hoped that Diane's dire omen was not coming true.

She sped up until she was pulling in front of the house, the pineapple-capped fountain gurgling pleasantly, the soothing sound welcoming her to the grand home.

Stan's car was in the opened garage, as was Christine's SUV. *Something had to be wrong*, Loretta told herself.

She found the key Christine had hidden in a flower pot, the key she told Loretta to use whenever she wanted.

Slowly, Loretta unlocked the door and stepped into the quiet foyer. The air was heavy and there was an odd, almost metallic odor.

She called out: "Christine? Stan?"

But she received no reply.

Curiously, she headed to the kitchen but stopped abruptly.

"Oh, my God! Christine!"

Upon first view, it appeared that someone must have gotten into the house, but as she drew closer, she could see that wasn't the case.

A gun was gripped in Christine's right hand, her body slumped forward, her face supported by the table top. The back of her skull shattered by the exiting bullet. A disgusting spray of bone shards, blood stains and brain material splattered across the kitchen floor and cabinet doors.

Immediately, she pulled out her phone and dialed 911. After she explained the scene, she had stumbled upon and urged that the police and ambulance get to the house as fast as possible, she headed upstairs.

When she saw Stan, she gasped. *Not possible*, she told herself.

Quickly she went to Michael's room only to find the same horrifying sight. Sadly, she knew what she was going to find in Maggie's room.

Sitting at the top of the steps, waiting for help, she asked herself over and over. "Why? How could Christine do such a thing?" Then she again remembered Diane's prediction. Suddenly, Loretta jumped to her feet.

The medallion, she thought. Diane had called it the nexus of evil.

Loretta hurried back to the kitchen, and without touching anything, she maneuvered around Christine's lifeless body. She could see no medallion, not even the chain that had been specially purchased for her precious piece. Christine would never have removed it. Loretta stepped back, confused and stunned. Just then she heard the ambulance arrive.

She called out that she was in the kitchen. The paramedics took one look and knew there was nothing they could do.

"Upstairs," Loretta whispered and then broke down in tears.

By the time the police arrived, Loretta had pulled herself, somewhat together. Several officers entered. She recognized a couple of them from working so long in the area. They acknowledged her with weak smiles and quick nods of the head.

When asked why she was there, in the house, she explained how she was friends with Christine, and how Christine had missed their weekly lunch date, something that just wouldn't happen. That's why she came by, to see if anything was wrong. Apparently, things were very wrong.

Yellow tape was stretched across the front entry way, as well as the back doors. An investigation would have to be completed before the bodies could be removed. Cause of death? Forceful entry? Burglary?

But Loretta knew how they died. Gunshot. There was no break-in, no thievery, just an inexplicable and horrendous tragedy. Although she did wonder, again, what had happened to the medallion. Regardless, she chose not to mention that to the officers.

When she was finally allowed to leave, she slipped under the yellow tape and headed to her car. Another ambulance had arrived as did three more police cars. Officers were combing the house for anything that might give them a clue as for the reasons why four people died.

She turned to look back at the house before climbing behind the wheel. More tears began to blur her vision. They'll find no clues, she knew. At least, nothing they could understand.

Arriving home, she knew there were phone calls to make. It really wasn't her responsibility, but Christine had been her friend and no other family existed in Florida.

First, she called the hotel and spoke to the assistant general manager. A gasp met her ear upon revealing the news, then silence. Loretta didn't go into detail as to the causes, she only said that there had been a terrible accident. The police could give them more details later. And if there are to be services, she would let them know that too.

Then she called Diane. Diane's message picked up and all Loretta could say was: "It's too late, Diane. Please call me."

Then she prepared herself for the hardest phone call of all— Christine's mother. Again, Loretta chose not to go into detail. Besides, she wouldn't have been heard over the sobbing at the other end.

"I knew something was wrong," the woman said. "I've been calling her all week and she never called back, not once." More sobbing.

"Let me know what you'd like me to do. Arrangements. Will you come down? Let me know." Loretta wasn't sure if she had even been understood, but she remained on the line until she heard an okay and a thank-you.

She put down her cell just as Matty came through the door. "What's the matter?" he asked, seeing his wife's red eyes and pallid complexion.

"Christine," she managed to say. "They're all dead." She broke into a renewed shower of tears.

Matty rubbed her back. "Oh, my God! What happened."

Loretta kept her eyes lowered to her lap. "I never thought I'd say this, but they got them."

"They?" Matty asked.

"Whatever is in that house." She wiped her nose with a Kleenex she found inside her purse. "Now it makes sense why no one stayed very long in that place."

Matty was struggling to suppress an I-told-you-so. It really wasn't the time. All he could say was, "I suppose there'll have to be disclosure for the next buyer."

Loretta looked up at him in shock. "Next buyer? I'll never go near that place, let alone try to sell it. I could never! If you ask me, that place should be bulldozed."

Chapter 19

Christine's mother arrived two days later. Loretta met her at the airport, only recognizing her by the photo Christine had once texted her. Upon meeting, Loretta learned her name was Charlotte.

They drove to the hotel where Loretta had arranged a room for her, for as long as she needed.

Once settled in, Loretta asked if she drank. Charlotte nodded. "I'm not a big drinker, by any means. But I could use one now."

"What do you prefer?" Loretta asked scanning over the In Room Dining liquor list.

"White wine, preferably," Charlotte replied.

"Good. Me too." She called down and ordered two bottles of chardonnay.

"Tell me what really happened," Charlotte suddenly asked. "The police just told me there was a shooting, a massacre, really, and they suspected, for now that Christine had done it."

Charlotte stepped to the window and looked out over the Gulf. Under any other circumstances she would be enthralled by the sparkling beauty of this tropical paradise, but she just stared at it numbly. "Christine and Stan were happy. The kids were happy. Where did she even get a gun in the first place?"

Loretta didn't know where to begin, but she tried, tried to ease in, to make this horrible news a little less horrible. "For protection, I think."

Charlotte turned away from the view and looked at Loretta. "From what? Was the area dangerous?"

"I think it was to protect against gators."

"Alligators!" Charlotte said with shock.

"The house sits near a swamp, the Everglades. A gator came out onto the lawn once. Stan thought it best."

Charlotte began to pace, then dropped into a chair. "She hated guns. Alligators? She never said a word about such a thing."

Loretta was becoming antsy for the wine to be delivered.

There was a knock on the door. *Finally!* Loretta thought.

A young waiter entered with an ice bucket and two bottles nestled inside. "Would you like me to open one?" he asked politely.

Loretta waved him off, adding a generous gratuity to the check she herself signed.

She found a wine key, popped open one bottle, and poured two glasses. Solemnly, they sipped, Charlotte in disbelief that any of this had happened at all, devastated that her daughter and her family were gone.

Loretta took a deep gulp, wondering how much she should tell Charlotte, that is, about the possible haunting, especially about the medallion that held an inexplicable yet powerful hold on Christine. And what Diane had said after visiting the property. But after a minute, she decided against saying anything. It would be of no use, especially if Charlotte was a skeptic about these things, just as she had been.

Instead, they sipped the wine chatting about memories, about the kids and Stan. "Good-looking man," Loretta blurted unexpectedly, probably powered by the wine.

"Yes," Charlotte replied. "Christine was very lucky to have met him."

Loretta eyed the now empty bottle. She stood and prepared herself to leave. "You must be exhausted, physically and emotionally."

Charlotte nodded then lifted her gaze. "I want to see the house."

Loretta wasn't really surprised by the request. From what she could only guess, the mansion on Hawk's Bend now belonged to her. She had a right. Nevertheless, she remembered what she had told Matty, about never setting foot in there again. The idea of what might be happening in there gave her a little chill. She certainly didn't want to be affected by any negative forces.

"I'll pick you up at ten in the morning. Is that good?"

Charlotte managed a weak smile. "Yes. And thank you for everything."

As Loretta waited for the elevator to return her to the lobby, she wondered if the forensic team had cleaned up the place. It would be too shocking for Charlotte to see the blood, bones, and brains of her beloved daughter and family. She, herself, certainly wouldn't want to endure such a scene if it had happened to anyone in her family.

While she waited for the valet to bring her car around, she dialed the local police station and asked to speak to either of the two officers who she knew. Fortunately, Eddy was working and took the call. She explained the situation.

"Sure, Loretta," he reassured her. "I'll check it myself. It won't be spotless, but it should be bearable."

She thanked him, terminated the call, tipped the valet and drove off toward home.

*****

Charlotte was waiting outside the hotel when Loretta pulled in, precisely at ten.

Dressed in a black skirt and a dark blue blouse, she appeared the epitome of somber and sorrow. "I just got down here. Good timing."

Although, she appeared to be in a mourning state, the tone of her voice belied it. To Loretta, it sounded almost chipper.

"Are you all right?" Loretta asked.

"Certainly," Charlotte replied, turning her head to gaze at Loretta. She returned her gaze back to the street ahead of them and sighed. "I guess I'm not very good at pathos. To be honest, this whole thing is killing me inside, but it just wants to stay hidden from public view."

Loretta pulled up to a stop sign, applied the brake, then slowly moved through the intersection. After another moment of silence, she re-assured Charlotte: "Please feel comfortable with me. Christine was becoming like a sister to me. Just feel free to express whatever you need."

Charlotte sighed, "Thanks."

"You've never seen the house, have you?" Loretta asked.

"Only from photos Christine texted me. The place seems very grand."

Without replying, Loretta remained silent the rest of the way although her mind was in a maelstrom of thoughts. Should she tell Charlotte what she knew, that the house was under some kind of haunting, or about the fixation Christine had on that medallion she found while gardening? She couldn't tell whether Charlotte would embrace the possibilities or regard them as mere hogwash.

Hawk's Bend was coming into view. The car swerved onto the private road and slowly pulled up to the portico.

A police vehicle was parked near the now closed doors of the garage.

Eddy, Loretta thought. Apparently, he was still inside.

They sat for a moment until Charlotte tugged on the door handle. She slowly climbed out and first, turned her attention to the fountain that gurgled merrily, then her eyes drifted to the police car, then turning she positioned herself to gaze up at the imposing entry way.

"A little like Tara," she said.

Loretta managed a smile. "Everyone thinks that. The original builders must have been fans of *Gone with the Wind*."

When they climbed the steps, Loretta realized she wouldn't need to use a key. The door was slightly ajar, and they could hear movement echoing in the abyss of the foyer.

Eddy called to them. "Come on in, ladies. All done here."

They stepped inside to find Eddy, decked out in his police uniform, holding a large trash bag, stuffed with who knows what. His expression was inscrutable. He first turned his attention to Charlotte. "My sympathies for your loss."

Charlotte managed a weak smile and thanked him.

Then his attention turned to Loretta. "Did the best I could."

"I can't thank you enough," Loretta replied.

Eddy and the trash bag slipped between them and disappeared out the door. Loretta excused herself and followed Eddy out onto the porch.

"Eddy," Loretta said in a low confidential tone. "Was there a medallion found? It was silver, twice the size of a silver dollar. Inscribed with Spanish words?"

Eddy shrugged and shook his head.

"Christine never removed it from her neck. I didn't see it either when I discovered her."

Eddy could only say that if anything like it shows up, he'll contact her.

Loretta thanked him again and rejoined Charlotte who was gazing around the foyer in the strangest way. Together, they waited until they heard the car drive off. Loretta locked the door and then proceeded to give Charlotte a tour.

"Shall we start upstairs?"

There was no reply. Charlotte obediently followed Loretta up the grand staircase. When they reached the landing, Loretta turned to see if Charlotte was all right. What she found was a woman, her arms outstretched, her palms turned upward, wearing the oddest expression.

"Charlotte?" Loretta whispered.

There was no answer. Her arms fell back to her sides and a confused Loretta continued to lead her down the hall to the master bedroom.

Fortunately, Eddy had seen that the bed was stripped of its sheets and pillowcases and anything else that might have been stained with blood. That was probably what was stuffed in the garbage bag.

Loretta allowed Charlotte the time to wander the room, stopping to gaze out the window to the pool and the yard beyond.

Then they made their way down the hall to the children's rooms. Their beds, too, had been stripped of the sheets and pillowcases. Nevertheless, Charlotte continued to display what Loretta read as unexplainable behavior: swiveling her head as if she was watching something fly through the room, stepping back as though getting out of the way of some invisible force, grabbing at her stomach as though she suffered a cramp.

"Are you all right?" Loretta asked with a little more urgency.

"This is a terrible place," was all that Charlotte could say.

They started back down the staircase and into the kitchen. Of course, it's a terrible place, Loretta thought. People were killed here!

Eddy had done a fine job of eradicating the visuals.

Once again, Charlotte quietly moved around the room absorbing the atmosphere that seemed heavy and suffocating. Then she found the door to the pool, slid it open and stepped outside into the warmth of the morning. She peered across the lawn, down to the swamp.

"They're there. Waiting," she suddenly blurted.

Loretta looked to where she thought Charlotte's gaze had alit but saw nothing. "Who's waiting?"

Charlotte turned to Loretta and suggested they sit. Each taking a chair poolside, Charlotte turned to Loretta and said: "I have a confession."

Loretta prepared herself. Confessions were not always pleasant things to hear.

"I can tell there is a lot of evil in this house and on this property."

Loretta couldn't speak. She was flabbergasted into silence.

"Christine never knew I had this…gift. If you want to call it that."

Loretta sat frozen.

"I think it came from my grandmother," Charlotte said as her eyes began wandering the property.

"If it's inheritable wouldn't Christine have this 'gift' also?"

Charlotte shrugged. "I'm told it usually skips a generation. I think Maggie may have had it but wasn't aware. And I'm certain Christine didn't have it. She lived in a haunted house for years and never knew."

Thinking back to previous conversations with Christine, Loretta remembered her saying that their old house made lots of sounds. "Haunted?"

"Yes," Charlotte replied. "But it was nothing more than a mischievous young boy who died on the property years before the family moved in. He was noisy but harmless. I couldn't have said anything to my daughter, she first wouldn't have believed me, and second, would have thought I was just a batty old woman." She felt a coolness pass over them. "There's something very evil, very ancient, and very angry on this land. I only wish now that I had visited earlier, so I might have been able to do something about it."

"Like a cleansing?"

"Yes." Charlotte turned and shot a surprised look. "You know about these things?"

"Not really. But after Christine told me all about the knockings and scratching in the walls, missing objects, furniture being moved, I contacted a medium named Diane. She said the same thing. Is this something you could do?"

"I don't know," Charlotte confessed. "This thing is strong, maybe demonic."

Loretta leaned back against the chair. Up until the time the family bought the house, she knew nothing about hauntings and spirits and vibrating medallions. Now Charlotte is talking about demons! How much more bizarre could it get?

Then Loretta remembered: "I assume since Stan had no family, this place is now yours."

Charlotte said nothing.

Then Loretta said something that surprised Charlotte. "There was a medallion."

Charlotte listened intently. "Go on."

"Christine found it while planting those fruit trees." She pointed to the far left, to a copse of young citrus trees. "She became obsessed with it."

"What kind of medallion was it?"

"It was silver and about this big," she formed a circle with her thumb and index finger. "She had it appraised. Apparently, the metal alone gave it considerable value. It was dated from the late sixteenth century, and she was told by a coin dealer that because of its historical value, could be worth much more."

"Were there any depictions on it? Letters?"

"As a matter of fact, it was Spanish and had three names inscribed on it. At first, Christine showed it off like a new baby, but in time, she wouldn't let anyone touch it. And she became very aggressive if you tried."

Charlotte took it all in.

"But the strangest thing was that it vibrated."

Now Charlotte's mouth dropped open.

"If you held it, it gave off the faintest of vibrations. Anyone who touched it could feel it. And she became so fixated on it that she had a chain attached, and she wore it around her neck day and night."

"Where is it now?" Charlotte asked.

"That's the odd thing. When I found her, it was gone. In fact, just before Officer Eddy left, when I stepped outside with him, I asked if it had been found by the police. He said nothing like that was found."

The coolness seemed to intensify. "Do you think it was stolen?"

"The police said there was no break-in. Everything was secure."

Charlotte pondered quietly what might have happened, why her daughter would murder her family as well as herself, if that's what she did. That's what the police believe, she knew. But Christine was a loving, caring mother and wife. She had been a schoolteacher. She was not an insane human being. None of it made any sense.

"I mentioned Diane. I brought her here just to look around, hoping she'd debunk everything. But of course, she didn't. She saw the medallion on Christine. Later, she said it was a nexus of evil."

Charlotte shook her head and emitted a deep sigh. "This just keeps getting worse by the minute." Then she asked, "What else did Diane say?"

Loretta thought to their ride back to the real estate office where Diane had parked her car. "She said there was some kind of struggle going on."

"Struggle?" Charlotte repeated. "What kind?"

"She didn't say. The only other thing she said was that the family was in danger. I even called her to come back ASAP, but she was out of town and wouldn't be able to return until this weekend."

"A little late," Charlotte said sadly. "I think," she said after a pause. "I think we need to find this medallion. It might be the answer to cleaning up this mess."

She paused then added, "It's said that things can vibrate because there is so much energy attached to them. It sounds like this medallion might very well be a nexus of evil."

"What should we do now?" Loretta asked.

"Well," Charlotte replied, "first, we'll need to search the house for that medallion. Then we'll wait for Diane and get some guidance from her."

Just as she finished speaking a gush of cold air whipped around them. It was so cold that the women shivered. A strange experience since the daytime temperatures were hovering in the eighties.

"They're watching us," Charlotte said.

They rose from their seats and moved back inside.

Loretta suggested that they begin with the bedrooms.

As they climbed back up the stairs, Loretta inquired about services. "Was there a plan?"

Charlotte rested for a moment, pressing her weight against the banister. She sighed deeply. "I've decided to have them cremated and their ashes returned to New York." She resumed her climb until they reached the second floor. "They asked me at the hotel about my plans. I told them as much. They want to have a memorial. I got the feeling Stan was well liked."

"Very much," Loretta said.

They reentered the master bedroom and began a search. Drawers were opened, closet shelves were investigated. They lifted the mattress, peeked under the bed. Charlotte rifled through the pockets of her daughter's clothing. Nothing. When they felt that they exhausted the possible places, they moved on to Michael's room.

Loretta found his iPad on the night table and recalled how he was never without it. A sadness overwhelmed her, and she suddenly began to cry.

Charlotte came to her and wrapped her comforting arms around her shivering body. She, too, began to weep. It seemed the emotions had built to a point that it was no longer possible to keep them inside. They allowed themselves several minutes to release the sadness, and then taking deep breaths, blotting their eyes with some tissue Loretta found in her pocket, they resumed their search.

Unfortunately, no success, so they moved to Maggie's room. As they stepped inside, they both stopped. Against the wall appeared a large black mist. It took form slowly revealing itself to be of human shape.

Loretta couldn't speak. She had never seen such a thing and she had never experienced such paralyzing fear.

"Leave this house!" Charlotte suddenly shouted. "You are not welcomed here."

Loretta was shocked to hear the power that was Charlotte's voice.

Then they heard a laugh, as if the thing was mocking them.

Again, Charlotte cried out: "Leave this house!"

It was followed by a voice that made their blood run cold: "Never!"

Together they moved backward, through the door and out into the hall.

The atmosphere of the house grew heavier and darker.

"Maybe we should save this room for later."

Loretta swiftly agreed. They descended the stairs and went to the kitchen. She spied a little blood splatter that had been absorbed into the oaken tabletop but tried to ignore it, maybe hoping that if she didn't see it, it wouldn't exist. Instead, they began to open cabinets and sliding open drawers but found nothing but dishes, glassware, and utensils. Loretta even peeked into the refrigerator but found nothing, except a few bottles of unopened white wine. She was dying to uncork one and have a glass if for no other reason than to calm her frazzled nerves. But she knew it would be in poor taste, so she shut the door and pretended she hadn't seen them.

Moving from room to room, they checked everywhere. Charlotte paused at the family photo that Maggie had seen tossed to the floor. Charlotte picked up the frame now missing the glass and gazed at her child, son-in-law, and grandchildren. She'd never be able to hold them, never enjoy holidays with them, never—she paused to think. Maybe that's what that creature upstairs meant when in snarled the word *never*?

She set the frame back onto the table and rejoined Loretta in the search, looking beneath sofa cushions, behind curtains, under chairs.

"I don't understand," Loretta finally said as she stood in the middle of the rec room. "Christine would never let that medallion out of her sight."

Charlotte glanced at her watch. "I think we've done enough here. Why don't we just take a break and have some lunch."

"And a glass of wine," Loretta added, through the first smile she had experienced all morning.

Loretta took Charlotte to the same restaurant she always lunched with Christine.

"It became our favorite place. We sort of bonded as friends here."

As usual a bottle of wine was served, salads were ordered, and the two women continued their discussion of the lost medallion.

"I just can't see how it could disappear so completely," Loretta said between sips of chardonnay.

Charlotte could only shake her head. She had no answers either.

Loretta leaned back in her chair, enjoying the light headedness brought on by the wine, "I think, after lunch, I'm gonna go over to the Collier County Historical Society. I want to see if I can get more information about the house and the land. There might be something that could help."

After lunch, Loretta drove Charlotte back to the hotel. "While you check history, I'm going to discuss a memorial service for the employees here. I'm certain they're afraid that they won't be able to pay their respects."

A lump formed in her throat as she realized the finality of it all. They were really gone forever. It was a difficult concept to absorb.

CHAPTER 20

As Diane's Nissan SUV sped west along route 75, otherwise known as "Alligator Alley," images of Hawk's Bend began to loom. She hadn't spoken to Loretta since their last conversation when she had to delay her return due to a family crisis. Now what she was feeling and seeing, made her realize she was facing another crisis, one of dire consequences.

She tried to shake off the visions by concentrating on the road that cut directly through the Everglades. At various viewing spots, tourists had pulled over to look out across the "sea of grass," hoping to spot one of the millions of gators that inhabited this marshland. Blue herons and snowy egrets fluttered overhead, while some took a perch on the railing that kept the viewer at a safe distance from the muck beyond. Children ran about the parking lot, chasing the birds that took roost on car hoods and between vehicles.

Eventually, the exit directing drivers off the highway and onto the road that would take her toward Naples came into view. The closer she got, the stronger the images. Without being told, she already knew a horrible end had come to the family. She just didn't know the details. Then an image, dark and ominous, came into her mind's eye. It was telling her to stay away. Don't come. Turn back. It was attempting to overwhelm her with dread. But she was experienced. She knew the tricks to quiet such evil things. She had dealt with angry spirits and demons in the past. She showed it no fear, but she could sense it to be powerful and she wondered how long she could keep it at bay.

Stopped at a traffic signal, Diane picked up her phone to text Loretta. She'd meet her at the house in thirty to forty minutes. The light changed to green, and Diane sped off in the direction of Hawk's Bend.

When she finally arrived, she spotted Loretta's car. Obviously, she had gotten the message. Exiting her vehicle, she stepped up to the fountain, it's endless splashing sending what should have been a calming feel. Instead, that dark thing was stronger, telling her again, and in no uncertain terms, to keep away. Do not enter the house. It was getting more difficult to resist it.

Stepping around the fountain, she climbed the steps and entered through the unlocked door.

"Loretta?" she called out in the emptiness of the foyer. The atmosphere inside seemed darker and heavier than it was the last time she had visited. Whatever was attempting to keep her away was growing in evil and power.

Two women appeared from the kitchen. Diane recognized only one.

"So good to see you," Loretta said, a little desperation invading her voice. Then she made introductions. "This is Christine's mom."

"Where is Christine?" Diane asked, certain she was going to regret the question.

Loretta's face dropped. "Let's go out back," she said as she led them poolside, offering them chairs.

Charlotte sat, but Diane preferred to stand.

Loretta began to tell the horrible tale of what happened the previous Saturday, of how Christine no-showed for their usual lunch date, of coming to the house, of finding not only Christine at the kitchen table, her head splattered with blood, but also upstairs, where the rest of the family lay murdered in their beds.

Charlotte knew Diane needed to know the events but was troubled by reliving them. Instead, she tried to block out Loretta's voice and focus on the copse of citrus trees, some now in full bloom. *Too bad*, she thought, *Christine would never taste the results of her plantings. There's that word again,* never. *How could one simple word create such angst?*

Suddenly, Diane's attention was drawn to the end of the lawn, to the line of palm and bramble that separated the manicured grass from the chaos of sawgrass and mud.

"What is it?" Loretta asked, noticing that Charlotte, too, was watching the same spot.

"It's them."

"Who?" Loretta asked impatiently. It seemed that everyone, except her, could see things. Then she reconsidered, maybe that was a good thing.

Diane pointed to the far right. "There are two of them. Their skin looks as if covered by sores and pock marks."

"Yes," Charlotte said. "I see them too."

Diane's head spun around to Charlotte, but before she could say anything, Charlotte said, "I also have a gift. I think, not as powerful as yours, but a gift all the same."

Now Diane sat. "This is definitely a wonderful thing."

Loretta, feeling a little left out, interrupted. "Before we continue, I found out a few things from the Historical Society." The two women turned their attention to what she discovered.

"This house was built by a wealthy German family who abandoned it after only a couple of years, and everyone who lived in this place also moved out fairly quickly."

"It sounds as if the problem is in the land," Diane suggested.

"Well, there's not a lot of documentation, but it is known that this whole area, from the north of Naples, south to the tip of Florida was inhabited by a tribe called the Calusa. Apparently, they weren't the nicest of peoples. There was also something I found in documents from the sixteenth century, that a large group of these people were wiped out by an epidemic of smallpox."

"That makes sense," Diane said. "The sores."

"My lord," Charlotte shuddered. "These spirits have been hanging around for almost five hundred years?" She looked at Loretta, "But what we saw in Maggie's room was no Indian."

Diane sat down. "What did you see?"

Charlotte attempted to describe how the ominous black cloud morphed into something of human form.

Loretta broke in, "It looked like a man, small stature, dark hair, beard, black eyes. And it laughed at us." A shiver ran across her. She wasn't sure if it was from the memory of the fear she had experienced or a change in the weather.

"Then," Charlotte added, "it growled out one word."

Diane leaned in.

"It said, 'Never!'"

Diane contemplated what they had told her. This was the evil she had been sensing earlier driving to the house. "I can't be certain, but I feel this is the real problem. I think that whatever or whoever this thing is, it's been here a long time, stewing in its anger and hate. I think it may be or becoming demonic."

"What does that mean?" Loretta asked.

"It means we've got problems." Then she remembered what Charlotte had just told her. "But there's two of us," she said, referring to Charlotte's gift.

"What am I?" Loretta asked. "Chopped liver?"

The tension broke, and the women broke into a stress-reducing fit of laughter. When they pulled themselves back together and wiped the tears that dripped from their eyes, Diane took Loretta's hand.

"Oh no. There will be plenty for you to do."

Chapter 21

The hotel had done a magnificent job memorializing Stan and his family. Chairs had been set up in the larger of the three meeting rooms, a buffet table covered with an assortment of hors d'oeuvres had been set up at the rear of the room, and a podium was situated at the front, facing the employees who came and left, some off for the day, others at work, popping in on breaks.

Loretta was shocked but pleased as to how many people came. There were employees who drove down from Palm Beach, who had worked with Stan, though only for a short while. She knew no one, but recognized faces from the yard party Stan and Christine threw not so long ago.

Someone, who identified herself as the assistant general manager of the hotel, went up to the podium, tested the microphone, assuring that it worked, then adjusting her pink-framed glasses, spoke.

She spoke of Stan's professionalism, his generosity to all, and his sense of humor.

Loretta squeezed Matty's hand, still amazed, that he dislodged himself from that chair, put on a clean suit and tie, and accompanied her. But her attention returned to the speaker as she called upon Charlotte to say a few words. The speaker identified her as Christine's mother.

Charlotte who sat to Loretta's left, reluctantly stood, and moved forward as a hush fell over the room.

Nervously, she approached the podium, thanked the assistant GM, and leaned into the microphone.

"I want to thank everyone for being here. I know my son-in-law and daughter would have been very appreciative. They were a wonderful family, and I was very proud of them all." Another lump formed causing her to hesitate. She certainly didn't want to lose her composure in front of all these people. Already, from where she stood, she could see some quietly sobbing, and heard the blowing of noses.

"I'm in shock, as most of you are, so you'll forgive me if this is short." She glanced over at Loretta. "But I'd like Loretta to come up and say a few words."

Loretta imagined strangling Charlotte. Public speaking was not her strong point. But considering it was the family and Charlotte, she stood up, and in spite of her shaking knees, she managed to make it to Charlotte's side. They hugged, and Charlotte left Loretta to herself.

Loretta peered out at the sea of faces that had grown since they had arrived only a half hour before. She cleared her throat.

"When I first met the family, I was their real estate agent. But in that short time, I was honored to become a family friend. And Christine and I were becoming the best of friends. Sisters. She was smart, funny, and there was nothing more important to her than her family. She adored her husband and doted on her kids."

Someone in the back of the room caught her eye. It was Ben. The boy who was interested in Maggie. She refocused and continued her impromptu speech.

"I will sorely miss her. And I know you, who knew Stan far better, will sorely miss him too. I can only guess that we're all better off from knowing them. Thanks."

Her legs still trembled as she left the podium. She made her way through the crowd and approached Ben. "Are you okay?" she asked.

He quietly nodded. "I can't believe it," he whispered as if stifling the urge to cry. "We really liked each other."

"I know," Loretta said. She looked over to Ben's parents who tried to return a smile.

"I know her Mom didn't want us to see each other."

"I know. Christine often talked about it." She placed her hand on his well-muscled arm. "Time will heal everything." She knew it was a trite and over used thing to say, but it was the best she could do. "Listen, she added. "If ever you want to talk, just call me." She reached into her bag and drew out a business card handing it to him.

"Thanks," he said, slipping the card into his pocket.

"Charlotte would like to leave."

Loretta turned to see Matty just behind her. She could see Charlotte standing by the door speaking to mourners, and beyond, out in the hall, Diane. Matty gave her a little tug on the arm.

"All right," she said. "I'm coming."

Before Matty pulled away from the front entrance to the hotel, Diane leaned into the passenger-side window. "I'll stay with Charlotte, and then in the morning, I have some things to get. We'll meet you at the house at about three, tomorrow afternoon."

Loretta nodded.

Diane withdrew her head from the window and escorted Charlotte back into the lobby.

"I wonder what she's planning," Loretta said, as the truck veered onto the street and began heading in the direction of their home.

She turned to her husband. "I was very pleased that you wanted to come today. I know you didn't know the family."

Matty stopped her. "Hey, she was your friend. It's the least I could do."

CHAPTER 22

After showing a few properties to some potential buyers, Loretta drove to Hawk's Bend. She knew she would be early, but she decided she needed some alone time to process everything that's been going on. One day, she was an average real estate agent; the next, she was some kind of ghostbuster.

Slowly pulling up to the porch, she remembered the enthusiasm Christine showed upon seeing the house. Watching her take countless photos, following her as she wandered from room to room, practically beside herself from the excitement of what could possibly be hers.

Loretta's heart dropped as she recalled that day, that she would never again open that front door and find Christine's happy face. And she'd always regret never again sharing a Saturday luncheon together.

She found the spare key, unlocked the lock, and pushed open the door. Everything was unnervingly quiet. The air was noticeably thick, the lighting muted as though the windows were covered in a layer of dust.

She checked her watch. It was just two.

Wandering into the kitchen, she spotted the refrigerator. Maybe that wine is still there. Pulling open the door, she was joyous. Not only was it still there, but there was also a second bottle behind it. Finding a wine key, she popped out the cork, and taking a glass from the cabinet nearby, she filled it. But before taking the first sip, she raised the glass up high: "This for you Christine. I will always miss you and never forget you. I hope you've found a better place." That said, she took a long, soothing drink.

A chilly breeze seemed to blow over her and the kitchen became quite cold. Suddenly, she had an urge to go out to the back. Taking the glass with her, she opened the sliders to the pool and stepped out into the sun. Her eyes scanned the property's boundary line, and when they fell on the palms and bushes at the far end, she was certain she saw someone standing in the shadows, intently watching her. Maybe this was the same vision Diane and Charlotte saw the day before. Then she spotted the fruit trees. Something compelled her to get a better look at them. She headed toward them, slowly, now acutely aware that she was being watched. Turning once or twice, she attempted to see if anyone was still in the brambles, but she saw no one.

Finally, she got close enough to see that the trees were blossoming in profusion. It was fruit Christine or her family would never taste. The fragrance from the citrus flowers was intoxicating. But she noticed one that seemed to be withering. As she stepped up to it, she saw that the leaves, or at least what was left of them, had shriveled, and turned brown. The branches seemed lifeless too. Then at the base of what might be called a trunk, she glimpsed something glittering just beneath a spot of disturbed earth. Curiously, she knelt and pushed the soil away. To her utter astonishment, it was the medallion.

How could it have gotten out here? she wondered. Maybe Christine had placed it there before she did what she did. What other explanation could there be?

Suddenly, Loretta found her empty hand reaching down to lift it from the earth and once all the dirt and grit had fallen away, it caught the sunlight and dazzled. It was truly beautiful, she thought, and just as intoxicating as the citrus perfume. Her hand sensed that strange vibration, and she attempted to drop it back to the ground, but she couldn't. As if it had magnetically stuck to her hand, it would not detach itself. It was as though her fingers were in spasm and could not pull away.

Startled, she stood upright staring at the thing, unable to take her eyes from it, that nexus of evil, as Diane had called it. The silver chain that Christine had bought for it dangled from the medallion.

Loretta found a flat piece of lawn on which to set down her wine glass, now freeing up both her hands. She stood, staring in awe at the gleaming silver, the Spanish words etched into it. Knowing that she should get rid of it or give it to the police, she knew that it would bring nothing but trouble. Instead, she took the chain and placed it over her head, the medallion dropping onto her chest. The vibration tingled her skin.

A strangeness surged through her body, something like electricity, something powerful. Her hand unconsciously went to it, her fingers embracing it, just as she had seen Christine do. The vibration grew stronger, the wind picked up and for an exceptionally warm day, the air became frigid. Her breath was a vapor cloud ejecting from her mouth and dissipating. Sounds, like growling, could be heard from the swamps. She turned and now saw them, three of them, pockmarked faces, breastplates made of shells and beads. They were as solid as the trees they emerged from. Long, dead Calusa, she knew. What did they want? Why were they still hanging around?

Oddly, she did not fear them. She clung more tightly to the medallion and stepped toward them.

"Never," she growled back.

Her own voice startled her. What was happening, she wondered. Anger filled her and she wanted to destroy everything and everyone. This was unlike her. She rarely became angry. But this anger did not seem to be hers. It was coming from the medallion. That she was sure of. Yet she could not bring herself to remove it.

Instead, she stepped even closer to the apparitions. Surprisingly, they stepped, or more accurately, floated back. The closer she got, the farther away they retreated, becoming less solid, until they disappeared altogether among the bramble and sawgrass.

A sense of victory now filled her, as though she had fought off her enemies and won.

In their place, another figure appeared, in the shadows and out of the direct sunlight. It was a short man, with a short black beard, and eyes that burned into her. His dress was from an ancient time, pantaloons and a waistcoat. This was the same phantom she and Charlotte had seen in Maggie's room. He smiled oddly at her, as though he was mocking her. Then the form faded, replaced by a small ball of light that, like a bullet, shot directly at her. She felt the impact. She became more transformed. Emotions, emotions that weren't hers: intense fear, utter sorrow, then anger. Her fingers massaged the medallion and a sudden and inexplicable feeling of love and loss crept over her. She thought she was going insane. She began to weep openly. Her body went limp, and she tumbled onto the grass, tears pouring from her eyes. She wept so loudly, that she didn't hear her name being called from the pool deck.

Charlotte and Diane had seen her from the house. They made a dash across the lawn and huddled down next to Loretta.

"What is it? Are you all right?" Diane asked.

Charlotte immediately assumed Loretta was having another delayed emotional reaction to the loss of Christine and her family.

Loretta was face down in the cool grass and when the women managed to turn her over, they gasped.

The medallion!

"Where did you find it?" Charlotte asked.

Loretta managed to point to the dying tree.

"Take it off!" Diane demanded.

Loretta raised her eyes that tightened and squinted back, eyes that no longer seemed to be her own, and shook her head. "It's mine."

Diane realized that those were the same words Christine had said when she showed it to her the day of her visit. Blood drained from her face. She knew they had a problem. A big and dangerous problem. Whatever this thing is, Diane knew it was trying to control Loretta, as it probably did with Christine, and the final result would not be pretty. She and Charlotte will have to be strong and united if they were to end this thing.

Diane looked over at Charlotte.

"I know," Charlotte said with no prompting. "We have a big job ahead of us."

They lifted Loretta to her feet and propping her beneath both arms they began to direct her back to the house.

"Wait!" Loretta shouted.

They stopped and gave Loretta her freedom.

Loretta retrieved the wineglass and took a sip. She seemed suddenly calm. Rejoining the women, they continued without incident back to the house.

Once, they entered, Loretta turned and stared at them. Her eyes were black, her face a twisted scowl. "Never!" she screamed.

Diane lowered her voice to a whisper. "Never, Loretta. We'll never take the medallion from you. Promise."

This seemed to placate Loretta, who took a seat at the kitchen table, her expression now inscrutable.

On the kitchen counter sat a paper bag. Diane motioned for Charlotte to bring it to her. Inside were the weapons she would use to fight off the evil that was inhabiting the house.

Diane closed her eyes suddenly. "It's here," she said. "Stronger than ever. I think it's become stronger with the deaths. It thrives on death. It's rejuvenated by it."

A shudder ran through Charlotte's body. To think that the deaths of her family had fortified the evil thing made her nauseous. Yet she knew Diane was correct. She could feel the entity too. Stronger, more dangerous, and it was trying to take over Loretta.

"It's trying to possess her," Diane said.

"Yes, I know. And there are others."

Diane closed her eyes and nodded. "I see it now. Those Calusa are trying to steal the medallion. That is the battle. Now they're all trying to claim it from Loretta."

Diane took the bag and emptied the contents onto the kitchen table. It contained candles, holy water, and sage. A bible. And an eagle's feather that had been a gift from a Seminole Indian shaman. All, except the feather, had been blessed by a priest. This would make these tools more powerful against evil. There was also a large box of salt.

Charlotte peered down at the items, only vaguely aware of the use Diane had intended.

Diane saw her expression. "Sage is used to cleanse the house. The salt that we'll sprinkle around the perimeter will keep evil from getting back inside."

Loretta seemed to squirm when she saw everything strewn out before her. "What's this?" she asked.

"A first-aid kit, you might say," Diane replied. She was certain a full possession had yet to be made so there was some hope that this entity had not taken over Loretta's body and mind completely. In her experience, she had witnessed demons entering human bodies and wreaking havoc on their minds. And once that happened, it might necessitate a priest's intervention.

Taking the holy water, she sprinkled some on Loretta.

"Stop!" Loretta hissed.

"You are not wanted here," Diane suddenly said in a loud authoritarian voice. "This is not your home!"

"Never!" It was a growl, clear as a bell, and thankfully, not arising from Loretta's lips. That made it certain that a possession was not yet complete. It was an oppression, the preliminary to a full possession.

Charlotte searched the kitchen as to where the voice might have come. But it seemed to have emanated from everywhere.

Now Diane felt she could focus on the house. A cleansing would have to be made. She looked at Charlotte, "Concentrate on light and love. You have power. Use it!" She took a bundle of sage that had been secured with raffia, pulled a lighter from her pocket and lit the dry leaves into flame. Blowing out the lick of fire, it began to smoke.

Diane explained to Charlotte that smoldering sage was an age-old remedy for purification. She swept the plumes across the medallion which still hung from Loretta's neck. "Only light and love is allowed here."

Loretta shuddered uncontrollably. "Never," she sneered.

With another sweep over the medallion, a loud bang from upstairs shook the house.

"Only love and light will remain in this house. Any malicious spirits are not welcomed here!" Her voice was reaching higher decibels. "Evil is not welcomed here!"

The kitchen cabinet doors flung open. Dishes began to fly across the room. Everyone ducked to avoid being struck.

"Only light and love will remain in this home." Diane kept repeating. Now Charlotte had joined in making their chant louder and stronger.

One of the empty kitchen chairs rose up and flew past them, landing in the rec room.

Diane began moving. Charlotte was close behind. Loretta remained in the kitchen, her face flat against the tabletop.

Banging came from every wall, the ceiling and even below their feet.

"It's angry," Diane said with a smile. "Very angry."

"And strong!" Charlotte added.

They headed to the rec room, then the office, the dining room, the foyer, all the while waving the smoldering wand of sage, all the while chanting that "Only love and light are welcomed."

Diane motioned for Charlotte to look upward at the top of the stairs. Two Calusa stared angrily back at them.

They began to climb the steps, smudging as they ascended. The Indians faded away. From one of the bedrooms came a loud crash.

Diane led Charlotte to the right, toward the room that was once Christine and Stan's. They entered to find a night table turned on end. Broken picture frames lay in splinters. Glass shards strewn across the floor.

A cold blast of air swept through the room. The women could see their own breaths as vapor clouds.

Charlotte was relieved to be with Diane, who obviously had more experience routing out evil entities. Except in contacting the little boy prankster that existed in Christine's old New York home and a few other affable spirits, she would never have the guts to face off with such an evil and dangerous thing. She was realizing now, the concentration, the commitment, and the fortitude it took to be an effective medium. This was going to be one huge lesson in honing her skills.

"It's moving," Diane whispered, as she led Charlotte out of the room and down the hall to Maggie's bedroom.

They entered and saw it. A black shapeless shadow, covering one of the walls. It undulated and wafted back and forth. Charlotte fearfully drew closer to Diane, who took the eagle feather and wafted the smoke directly at the threatening entity.

It instantly disappeared, but not without first shattering the full-length mirror attached to the closet door. More banging from inside the walls. The mansion seemed to be alive.

"Only love and light are welcomed here. All evil must leave!" They began repeating in unison. Once, twice, three times.

Suddenly, everything became quiet. The room seemed brighter. The pressure alleviated.

Was it gone?

Turning, they headed, out into the hall and down the stairs. The foyer seemed brighter, the atmosphere less heavy.

Suddenly, they both realized Loretta had been left alone. They flew down the staircase and darted to the kitchen. She was gone. They called for her but there came no acknowledgement.

"There she is!" Charlotte shouted, spotting her through the window. She pointed out into the yard. "Down by the swamps."

The women rushed outside, calling out to her. Loretta, seemingly unaware of the women in pursuit, kept moving, approaching the palms and the wild bushes that made up the barrier. She reached a small opening and disappeared.

"Oh, my God!" Charlotte screamed.

And they saw that they were back, the Calusa, three of them. They did not stare up at them but watched Loretta and the medallion move farther out where the water and muck became deeper and more dangerous.

Charlotte paused for a moment and pulled out her phone. She dialed 911 and quickly explained their crisis, omitting the paranormal part, then shoved the phone back into her pocket. She caught up with Diane who had just broken through the bushes and began to follow Loretta into the sea of mud.

"Loretta!" they both screamed. They could just make her out ahead, trudging through the sawgrass and the small shrubs that grew in haphazard clumps, slogging through the knee-deep water, the mud sucking at her feet. They could also see the misty forms of Calusa pursuing her. Then another dark form appeared.

"It's him," Diane whispered. "The evil one." She suddenly had a vision. "I see now! The two forces are engaged in a battle. A battle…" she hesitated, "for the medallion!"

Loretta was in dire peril.

Loretta forged ahead. She was barely conscious. Nor did she have any idea where she was going or why. She could only hear a faint whisper in her head to keep going and not to stop, no matter what happened.

So she slogged farther and deeper into the water. She had felt her shoes sucked off her feet by the mud, and the burning cuts from the sawgrass, their serrated ridges as sharp as razor blades.

The women continued in pursuit. It didn't look good; they couldn't keep up. They both feared that Loretta would be lost out in the swamp, or worse, die!

Then they heard something, voices, calling out from beyond.

It sounded like human voices, coming closer. Then it came into view, a small canoe, with two men holding oars, guiding the boat toward them.

"Out there," Diane shouted. "There's a woman out there!"

The canoe shifted direction and glided along the path that Loretta had taken.

It seemed like hours, but it was fifteen minutes later, that the canoe reappeared. Loretta sat, slumped between the two men, filthy and covered with mud, her hair matted, her eyes barely open, peeking through what looked like a facial mask.

As they came closer, they could see that the two men were native Americans, their hair, long and held off the forehead by colorful bandanas.

They got as near to Charlotte and Diane as the water level would permit, then climbed out of the boat, lifting Loretta out also, and her near lifeless body into the shallows, and onto the lawn. There they laid her gently on the grass and waited to see if she was breathing. After a few anxious seconds, her chest heaved upward, a little water dribbled from her mouth onto her chin and her eyes opened wide.

"What?"

Charlotte shushed her and ordered her to be still.

At that moment they heard the siren of the paramedics' van pull in front of the house and two white uniformed ETs come running along the side of the house and across the lawn.

No one had to say anything. The ET's immediately administered oxygen and asked what had happened, why Loretta was covered in mud.

"She ran out into the swamps." It was all Diane could say.

"Did she have a reason to do so?" the older looking medic asked.

"None that we know of," Charlotte responded.

"Look we're going to take her to the hospital for observation. Are you related to her?"

"No, but we'll call her husband," Charlotte said. She turned to Diane. "I'll go to the hospital with her."

One of the medics had run back to the truck and returned pushing a gurney. They lifted Loretta onto it, strapped her down and together, maneuvered her a back across the grass, disappearing around the front of the house. Charlotte followed close behind.

Diane then turned to the two saviors. "Thank you so much," she said. "This could have turned into a disaster if it hadn't been for you."

They managed smiles and one of them asked, in hesitant words, "Are you aware that this land has a reputation for strange activity?"

Diane froze.

"Historically, this has been sacred land. But over the years, this fact has gone unnoticed or ignored."

"What were you doing out there?" Diane managed to ask, maybe to avoid talking about all the paranormal occurrences that have been happening.

"Fishing," they responded. "We come out in this area from time to time.

Diane couldn't resist any longer. "Do you ever see them?"

There was no hint of shock or misunderstanding in their expressions. She knew they knew what she was talking about.

"The Calusa?"

Diane nodded.

"Oh yeah. They lived in this area many hundreds of years ago. Controlled most of the western peninsula of Florida. They were called the 'fierce ones' or 'the shell people' because they liked to engage in battle and they were fishermen, like us. Lived mostly on seafood. Used the shells as decoration, much as many tribes use beads."

"But do you see them?" Diane insisted.

"Yeah, they're here. But the spirits we come across look deformed and sick. They appear to have pockmarked faces. But the apparitions fade quickly. We offer our respect to them. They do us no harm. It was their land. They have a right to remain."

"I suppose so," Diane conceded. "But there is another entity here too. Not Indian. It's evil and very strong."

The two men exchanged glances. "How do you know?"

Diane said, "I am a medium. I am in tune with the spirit world much like one of your shamans, I assume."

Both men nodded in understanding.

"There is some kind of battle being engaged here. I think that's part of the reason Loretta was lured into the swamps. Both sides wanted something from her."

Suddenly, she remembered that she didn't see the medallion around Loretta's neck. Unless it had slipped beneath her blouse and was hidden, it had fallen from her or ripped away by one of the powers. And if it fell off, and became part of the swamp, it would just have to stay there. At least it was outside the boundary of the land and house. Maybe some peace will now prevail.

"Don't underestimate spirits," one of the men said. "They can be very powerful, especially if angered."

"Whatever happened to the Calusa?" Diane asked.

"We know very little, except what I have already told you. It is thought that their multitudes were decimated by the White man's diseases. They had no immunities to typhoid, smallpox, and gonorrhea. It is thought that the few who survived blended in with other tribes or left Florida altogether for Cuba. They left no written records, no histories. Only speculation. They may have had many more secrets. But we'll never know."

The quiet of two looked to the sky. "It's late. We have to go."

"I hope your friend will be all right," the other said.

With that, they turned and disappeared back into the swamp to where their canoe waited.

Diane could barely hear the splash of their oars as they faded away.

Diane looked up at the house. Everything seemed quiet, for now. Maybe the cleansing had some affect. Maybe it was only a temporary stop gap. Only time would tell. But now she needed to seal the house with salt. She retrieved the box and walked around the exterior of the building, sprinkling as she went, making sure that the whole building was protected.

Back at the hospital, Loretta was cleaned up and examined. She seemed almost embarrassed when Charlotte entered her room. "No worse for wear," she said with a broad smile.

"What happened?" Loretta asked.

They waited until the nurse had left the room.

"You don't remember?"

Loretta shook her head. "I only remember a voice, inside my head, telling me that I should go into the swamp. To find them. To vanquish them." She touched her chest. "It's gone, isn't it?"

Charlotte shrugged. "You had it in the kitchen, but it was gone when we got you out of that horrid place."

"I saw them. I finally saw them," she said with some excitement.

"Who?"

"Those Indians."

Charlotte nodded slowly. "Yes. How many did you see?"

"Three," she said. "Their faces were horribly scarred. They came very close to me, one of them reached out as if he wanted to touch me. Then I heard the voice in my mind grow louder. 'Run,' it said. So I guess I ran." She thought for a second. "How did I get here?"

"Two men in a canoe magically appeared from nowhere. They pulled you out. The paramedics had already been called. I also called your husband."

Just as the words left her lips, Matty came flying into the room. "What the hell happened? Are you all right?"

Loretta broke into a smile. "Yes, I'm fine." He was obviously beside himself with fright. She liked the sudden way her lazy-ass husband was doting on her, frightened for her, caring about her. Oddly, it was an unfamiliar but very attractive feature he was demonstrating. A feature she hadn't seen since the early days of their marriage.

He pulled a chair up to the side of the bed, sat, and took her hand into his.

Charlotte excused herself and went out into the hall to call Diane to give her Loretta's progress.

A few hours later, the doctor released Loretta into her husband's care. Together, they drove back home in Matty's beat-up Ford truck.

Diane met Charlotte at the hospital not long afterward and returned to the hotel. Safe and comfortable, Charlotte poured a glass of wine. Diane reminded her that she didn't drink; instead, she accepted a bottled water.

Diane stared down at the plastic bottle. "I don't think the cleansing was strong enough. I don't think it worked."

Charlotte said nothing.

"I spoke to those two men who rescued Loretta. Native Americans, Daniel and William. They told me that they see the spirits of the Calusa in the swamp often. Said that it was their land. They have a right to be there." Diane lifted her eyes away from the bottle and looked at Charlotte. "They're probably right."

"So," Charlotte began to ask, "that place will never be safe?"

Diane thought for a minute. "Maybe if a shaman came to bless and purify the land. Maybe that would work."

"What about the other entity. That's the biggest problem, I think."

Diane nodded. "Maybe a house exorcism." She took a sip of water. "What are you going to do with the house?"

Charlotte sighed and thought for a moment. "Well, I couldn't unleash that place to someone else. That wouldn't be right. Fortunately, Stan took out life insurance on everyone. With the kids and Christine gone, I'm the sole beneficiary. I'm sure Christine's death will be marked as a suicide, and her coverage will be nullified. Nevertheless, there should be enough to keep the house in my possession for some time. Or at least, until I figure out what to do."

"Whatever, I'm just a phone call away. Maybe we can arrange that exorcism in the future. I have a priest friend who can come down with me and help us out. Just keep in touch and let me know when it's convenient."

"I appreciate that. Very much. You've really helped me through this. To see what was really going on. Especially, to know that Christine wouldn't have done what she did if that evil wasn't there."

Diane stood and gave Charlotte a bear hug. "Well, I suppose I should get on the road. My old man will be wondering where I've been."

As she saw Diane to the door, she smiled to herself. She thought Diane was gay.

CHAPTER 23

Charlotte rose early, ordered some coffee and toast through room service, then showered and packed her bag. Although everyone in the hotel had been more than gracious and generous, she felt she had overstayed her welcome and needed to leave. Besides, there wasn't much else she could do. Taking the elevator to the lobby, she was met with the bell captain who offered to take her bag. But she refused. It was light.

Then she stopped at the front desk to thank everyone for their kindness and support. The general manager had been notified that Charlotte was leaving so she hurried to the lobby to personally say her goodbyes.

"It was a pleasure meeting you. We're so sorry under such conditions, though."

Charlotte smiled. "I need to settle my bill."

The now GM shook her head. "No, no. This is my pleasure. Stan would have done the same if anyone else had gone through the same thing."

Charlotte thanked her and slowly walked to the door.

"Do you need a taxi?" one of the valets asked.

"No, thanks. A friend is picking me up."

No sooner as she had said that Loretta's car pulled under the porte-cochere.

Charlotte climbed in and off they went.

"There's still some time before my flight. Do you think…"

Loretta cut her off. "That's why I came early. I know you want to stop at the house one more time."

Charlotte smiled and sat back.

They pulled into the drive, parking close to the fountain that probably was short a few gallons of water. "It's got a whole different feeling now."

"Yes," replied Charlotte. "Not as welcoming."

"Should I wait here, or would you like me to come in with you?"

"No, no. I'll be fine. And I'll only be a minute. Just want to pay my final respects."

Loretta understood.

Charlotte shut the passenger door while Loretta kept the car engine running. The day was warming up. The air conditioner was a necessity.

Charlotte stepped into the foyer and sighed deeply. But her instincts began to register something. There was energy in the house, energy she hadn't noticed before. Sadness hung around her. Also, fear.

"I'm here to say goodbye, my loves." Her gut tightened and though she tried, tears still welled up. She took a tissue from her purse and dabbed at her eyes. Suddenly, she heard a faint sobbing. Uncertain from where it came, she began to move toward the kitchen. It grew louder as she approached.

She glanced around, but there was no one. Then she saw her. A hazy form stood at the kitchen window, facing out, apparently staring at the lawns beyond.

This was the source of the sobbing. Although Charlotte couldn't see the face, she knew it to be Christine.

A small gasp escaped her. Even in death, Charlotte couldn't bear to see her daughter so miserable.

"Christine," she called out, almost in a whisper. But there was no response. Only more sobbing.

It was clear that her soul had not crossed over to the other side or went into the light or wherever it was the dead go. She was trapped. That was the fear she had been sensing. And the sadness. She stood quietly wondering what she could do. Obviously, Diane had been correct. The cleansing they had done with the smudging of sage had little effect. Was her daughter to be trapped here forever? As she considered the situation, the vision began to fade, from practically a solid mass to an ethereal wisp to nothing at all. The sobbing had ceased too. But Charlotte's worry did not end. She turned and slowly made her way to the foyer. The sadness began to weigh upon her. Each step became an endeavor, as if she were walking through a room of water. Something caught her eye and she peered up at the top of the stairs.

"Oh God!" she gasped. There stood Stan and the two children staring back down at her, all wearing expressions of deep sorrow. But they appeared for only a blink of an eye. Suddenly, a dark amorphous cloud swept across the balcony. Her family had vanished with it.

Charlotte understood now. That evil entity not only continued to lurk throughout the house, but it was also entrapping her family. How could they move on and how could she free them?

In a loud voice, she called out to them. "I'm coming back!"

Diane was correct. An exorcism will have to be done. She'll call and arrange another day when she would fly back down and have Diane meet her at the house.

Moving as fast as the atmosphere would allow her, she stepped out into the sunlight where the world became once again normal.

Loretta could see Charlotte's expression.

"What happened in there?"

Charlotte took a deep breath. "I'm not sure," she replied.

"Well, something happened. I can see it on your face."

"I saw Christine."

"What?" Loretta shrieked.

"She's still there. So are Stan and the kids."

"You're kidding me!"

"I would not kid about something so serious. This damned gift of mine. It's not a gift at all. It's a curse!"

Loretta swerved onto the main road and began the trip to the airport.

"I think that evil thing is keeping them trapped." She dabbed her eyes with the tissue that had become crushed in the palm of her hand. "I don't know what to do."

Loretta remained quiet for a few miles, then spoke up. "Listen, I'll call Diane. We'll figure this out. We'll get them out of there."

Loretta had to remind herself that she was speaking about dead souls, not living and breathing people. She shook her head, amazed as to how her thinking had changed through this ordeal. She wished she hadn't been the agent who sold that house to Christine and Stan in the first place, then she wouldn't be involve in any of this. Yet as she glanced over at Charlotte, who slumped forward in her seat, appearing for the first time like an old woman, she smiled. If she hadn't sold the house, she wouldn't have had such a wonderful experience of knowing Christine and her family, and she wouldn't have been taken on an adventure, though as horrible as it has been, that still seemingly, had not yet ended.

When she finally got home after dropping Charlotte at her terminal for her flight back to Syracuse, she stepped into the house only to be met by Matty.

He stood before her dressed in a suit and tie, his hair combed and gelled, his shoes glistening with fresh polish.

"Holy crap! What's with you looking all dapper?"

Matty smiled, "I've got a few job interviews today. Maybe something will work out. Maybe I'll get busy and not be able to watch any more *Bonanza* marathons on the Family Channel."

Loretta actually felt sorry for him. What would his life be not catching up on the adventures of Hoss and Little Joe and all the other denizens of the Ponderosa Ranch.

She smiled and gave him a hug. "I'm not only impressed, but I'm also very proud of you."

For the first time in a long time, he leaned in and gave her one of the most passionate kisses of their marriage. "I love you. And I'm very proud of you. You're a brave woman."

She watched him climb into his Ford truck and disappear. *Maybe*, she thought, *He's not such a lazy-ass after all.*

About the Author

Patrick Olesko, born and raised in upstate New York, earned a degree in literature at Canada's Concordia University and became obsessed with the paranormal after his own frightening experiences. *The Medallion* is his first novel.